My dear
friend

May my
words
continue
to make
your
life
brewed
life
more
extraordinary

Love you
[signature]

St. George Press

Life~Lust and Love

THE SECRET MEMOIRS OF AN ORDINARY WOMAN LIVING AN EXTRAORDINARY LIFE!

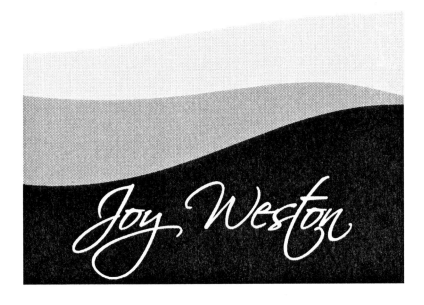

Joy Weston

First printing 2015

ISBN 978-1505382761

LCCN 2002100924

ATTENTION CORPORATIONS, COLLEGES, BUSINESSES, AND PROFESSIONAL ORGANIZATIONS: Quantity discounts are available on bulk purchases of this book for educational, gift purposes, or as premiums for increasing magazine subscriptions or renewals. Special books or book excerpts can also be created to fit specific needs.

For information, please contact Joy Weston at PO Box 25322, Sarasota, FL 34277.

CONTENTS

DEDICATION

This book is dedicated to all the women in the world who are committed to being the *Shero's* of their own life story...and to all the men who support them on their journey.

ACKNOWLEDGMENTS

One can never accomplish anything of great value by doing it alone, and even though it sounds redundant, since you probably have heard it a million times, it's true. But nothing brings that truism home more than when you take on a project that is by its nature is a solo activity: such as running a marathon, swimming the ocean to reach another shore, fighting off a potentially killer disease or writing your next "best seller."

Granted, much of the hard work can only be done by you and can only be accomplished by staying with your commitment to do what you say you are going to do, and not stopping till you reach your desired destination. But the best can't do it without help, and will not only admit it, but also joyfully give credit to all their special angels.

So in that vein I would like to begin by thanking sweet Orshi, for helping me look so good, my adored expert proof readers, Nancy Rego, Principal of Rego Interiors (RegoInteriors.com), and Lynne Strong, for helping me look even better on the pages of my book. Love ya!

To all of my loving supportive caring friends who continuously cheered me on and acknowledged my "stick-with-it-ness," something the celebratory me was often challenged with during the writing process; you know who you are and how much I love and appreciate you. From that pack, two people rose above and beyond the call of duty and I'd be remised if I didn't especially thank them for always being a Yes, to my unending creative requests.

Robert W. Hendrickson, III, Esq. one of the finest lawyers in Florida and possibly the world, thank you so, so much for taking your precious off hours and stepping in when my original editor bailed with all your wise insights and excellent editing skills. Without your assistance I would never have met my deadline, felt as assured in the flow of my words or enjoyed the experience half as much. For that, my dear "Bobby" I am eternally grateful.

Chad Thompson, founder of SYQ Music Television (syq.tv / syqtv.com) and Indie Fan, A World of Independent Media (indiefan.tv / indiefan.org). What an angel God sent me when you were dropped into my lap! Between your amazing talents and open hearted willingness to roll with my "creative" ideas and then to help me realize them, was a dream come true. You have been there every single step of the way, always encouraging me to keep expressing my vision and making sure that it was actualized. Thank you so much!

And lastly, let me acknowledge *You* my readers and loyal audience. Without you, my message and all my hard-work would be just sitting on a shelf collecting dust! But thanks to you, I am realizing my greatest dreams of all: Spreading the message of JOY and helping others learn the ways to turn their everyday ordinary anything...into their everyday Extraordinary Everything! Trust me, you couldn't give me a greater gift, and for that I thank you with all my heart.

Joy

LIFE ~ LUST ~ and LOVE...
OPENING THOUGHTS

"Follow your bliss and the universe will open doors for you where there were only walls."

Joseph Campbell

As I look at this empty page I am saying to myself, "what do I really want my readers to know about why I chose to write another book?" How deeply do I want to delve into the reasons and rhyme for making the decision to pull myself out of my blissful celebratory life and submit my mind, body and soul to the solitary existence of a writer for months on end? Why we do what we do is a complicated and interesting question, but even more so when we are making a choice that could drastically change our life not just in the moment, but potentially forever.

Upon introspection, my answer was more complex than I had even realized. My initial response was that within my commitment to "walk my talk," was this deep-seated aspiration to recreate a similar experience as I have with my *Pay it Forward Angels Network:* a private foundation I created to give women going through difficult times free copies of my inspiring

1

books. Now I have an overwhelming desire to spread JOY and empower women to become the *SHERO* and men the *Heroes* of their own life story, so we can all positively affect others and the energy in the world.

By emulating the mindset of *Paying it Forward*, I have to surrender some of *the best* of the savvy secrets I've garnered over the years for being *The Best* you can be to have *The Best* life ever! Life changers rolled into little vignettes about my amazing role models and mentors that I give full credit to for paving the way for living an Extraordinary life. Thanks to their shining example and astute tips, I have become the *Shero* of my own life story and sincerely hope to do the same for you!

As you will come to understand if you read any of my books, watched or listened to any of my programs, come to any of my varied workshops, presentations, forums or place that I speak, I believe to my core; to turn your ordinary *anything* into an Extraordinary *Everything,* is first and foremost Mind over Matter. Understanding and then utilizing this absolute truth properly, is all you will ever need to get to wherever, have whatever and whomever you want and deserve.

The time it took to prepare this offering wasn't as easy or effortless as my overactive fantasy mind hoped and thought it would be. But the deeper I got into it and the more meat I put on the skeleton of my vision, the closer I got to my joy. I could "hear" as the words landed on the paper what a soul and spirit changer this book was going to be and that gave me the impetus to figuratively chain myself to the computer yet another day.

It's been over a decade since I first wrote *How an Ordinary Woman Can Have an Extraordinary Life: The Formula for The Art of Living Well* that I am very proud to say, as of this writing is now in 14 languages and 22 countries. But way before its publication and certainly every day since, I have used these life lessons to positively affect and influence the outcome of my everyday life.

In that observation I realized that not only have my "words of wisdom" stood the test of time and created a strong foundation for living a life beyond my wildest dreams, but to truly make a difference in the world you must *always* practice what you preach, have the courage to be your genuine authentic self, and share the gifts you have been blessed with or received from others.

My intention for this book is to bring you behind the proverbial curtain into the private world of women who often are seen as enigmas, because of their captivating and mysterious ways. For you to feel the excitement of stumbling upon the private journal of a special sort of collector, someone that appreciates the rare, beautiful and unique; the cherished possession of one who values and highly respects the gifts of quality.

As with all private collections, there will be some stories that you will feel were written just for you and then there will be others you might not personally relate to at all. Those are probably the ones that will be just perfect for you to share with your BFF, mom, sister, daughter, niece, co-worker or a new friend that happily and auspiciously has just come into your life.

While composing these mini-novellas, I've tried my best to make them entertaining, titillating, enlightening, amusing, empowering, even a bit naughty and nice. Because these are my own private memoirs of narratives and antidotes that have influenced my life in *the best* of ways, once I acquiesced to sharing my secrets, I then full-heartedly held the same intentions for you.

I wrote this book because I truly believe that when each person can become the hero and *SHERO* of their own life story, you will then organically become part of the force that can turn the tide of a toxic negative energy into a peaceful and loving world~ and we can't have enough of that good energy, can we?

At your leisure, please do let me know if I've been fortunate enough to have accomplished even a small part of my vision. (Contact info in the back of the book) That would certainly put the *bliss* in my day!

En-JOY!

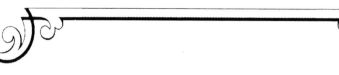

"What if you gave someone a gift, and they neglected to thank you for it - would you be likely to give them another? Life is the same way. In order to attract more of the blessings that life has to offer, you must truly appreciate what you already have."

Ralph Marston

LIFE

"Life is a song - sing it. Life is a game -play it. Life is a challenge - meet it. Life is a dream - realize it. Life is a sacrifice - offer it. Life is love -enjoy it." In all my searching, this quote is the closest to the way I have always felt. Except to add that *Life is a JOY - live it!*

Life, as I see it, is an incredible adventure to be experienced through all of our five senses; sight, touch, taste, smell and hearing. Each a portal to the seat of your soul and yet another opportunity to get a glimpse of your unique calling. There is a purpose to everything and everything has a reason for being. Living life, opposed to just being alive, is clearly about experiencing love and joy and every emotion that can awaken your senses. Then use all that knowledge to create *The Best Life* ever. Life isn't about finding yourself. It's all about creating yourself, a task only you can do.

"Our subconscious minds have no sense of humor, play no jokes and cannot tell the difference between reality and an imagined thought or image. What we continually think about eventually will manifest in our lives."

Robert Collier

THE FORMULA

"We are shaped by our thoughts; we become what we think. When the mind is pure, joy follows like a shadow that never leaves."
Buddha

THE FORMULA...my greatest ever epiphany and the foundation for all my work, is the one thing that has truly guided and defined all that I am most proud of these days. When the veil was finally lifted and the mystery of creation was exposed to me, in the form of *The Formula*, it was over-whelming. If I hadn't been at my own wedding...therefore obliging me to interact with many guests and act fairly normal...I think I would have been grabbing everyone like a zealous devotee.

In my book called *How an Ordinary Woman Can Have an Extraordinary Life: The Formula for The Art of Living Well,* I described my awakening by saying that, "In every person's life there is a moment in time when the clouds open up and the sun breaks through and a brilliant light shines down onto something that was so important, you can't imagine how you didn't see it sooner. Suddenly, *everything* becomes crystal clear and you now understand it all."

I went on to describe how this came to pass (but you need to get that book to read all the juicy details) and the realization that every man and every woman living on this planet creates their lives by following a specific formula. Whether the steps of *The Formula* are used positively or negatively is what will determine the experience and the quality of your life.

- *By the Thoughts That You Focus on...*
- *By the Words That You Speak...*
- *Your Actions and Reactions...*
- *And Whether or Not You Believe...*
  You Deserve To Have What You Really Want...
  Is How You Create the Experience and the Quality of Your Life.

Right smack in the middle of this very special day that was over-flowing with love and beauty, I was stopped with a Kaleidoscope of images from my past and present exploding in my head: All my successes and failures, my audacious over-the-top accomplishments to the most embarrassing ones I'd rather not mention. In what seemed like nanoseconds, my entire life flashed before my eyes and I saw how I used each step of *The Formula* to bring forth, create, design, and determine the quality of each and every single experience, and ultimately the tapestry of my life. WOW. Talk about mind-blowing!

This moment in time, this life-altering epiphany changed my life forever, and nothing has ever been the same. Knowing this to be the absolute truth, it's really impossible to pretend that you don't have any influence or power over the circumstances of your lives.

You might not be able to change the details of a situation or your past, but you certainly can change the outcome by how you think, speak, act and react to it. And most importantly, how you believe you can and will affect the experience and quality of your life.

I can't stress enough the importance of always being consciously aware of how you are using *The Formula* to create the life you want, need, desire of having, and in your heart know you can't settle for less. The gravity of staying diligent to never letting any of the circumstances of your so called "reality" deter you from realizing your dreams, can't be emphasized enough; especially since there really is no such thing as *reality*. It's been proven that each of us experiences a different reality at the same exact moment, depending on our own personal history and what's going on in that moment. So whose reality is the "real" reality?

Everyone has experienced having an expectation about how things are going to turn out, only to realize a completely different outcome, both positively and negatively. So if you agree that this is true, can you now also see how vitally important it is to create your own script and then to positively use each step of *The Formula* until you've manifested your vision?

Understanding and utilizing THE FORMULA is truly my greatest tool and my *secret* weapon, for turning anything ordinary into my *Everything* Extraordinary!

Here's how it works:

Start to think about something that you really, really, really want, and I mean *really, really, really want.* Because if you don't really, really, really want it, all the efforts that follow are going to feel like a lot of work and possibly fall short, instead of just one more step getting you closer to your dream.

It could be to find your ideal soul mate or life partner, accomplishing the seemingly impossible, reaching a career goal, enjoying perfect health or a fit, tone strong body. Maybe it's realizing a financial freedom fund or a level of abundance and prosperity that allows you to do whatever you want, not just what you can afford. Or it could be a montage of all of these things that creates a beautiful tapestry of your life. Whatever it is, make sure it is something that you really, really, really want, so you have the stamina necessary to stay the course. Once your vision is truly deeply embedded in your heart and you have aligned your full intentions upon your dream, begin to infuse it with the positive steps of *The Formula.*

The Thoughts You Focus on...

The thoughts you focus on do become things. The things that you think about over and over again and what and how you think about these various things, *absolutely* will create the experience and the quality of your life. Right now you may believe that most of your thoughts do serve you. But what I know from personal experience, is that if you were to step back and observe what you are repeatedly saying to yourself and what you're thinking about all day long, you'd be shocked at how often your thoughts are contradictory and even potentially damaging to what you "say" you really want. Just because in life you didn't get what you asked for or wanted, doesn't mean you didn't get what you were thinking about.

Thought transcends matter, *absolutely.* So to become consciously aware of what thoughts you are focusing on throughout the day is essential.

Amazing unexpected things can happen once you become a diligent watchdog over your daily thought process. Just keep checking in to make sure that your thoughts are positively focused on seeing your dreams manifested...and if they're not... immediately reframe those thoughts to serve you.

This is the great secret of some of the most successful and happiest people in the world. Follow their lead and one morning you will wake up to suddenly realize that you are now living the life you have always dreamed about, in ways that were never even on your radar! Focus on this one thought, and then start planning on celebrating all your extraordinary results.

The Words You Speak...

The words you speak are nothing more than an audio version of what you are thinking. Want to know what you are really thinking about any particular situation or person? Listen very carefully to what you are saying out-loud about everything. Whatever comes out of your mouth is your thoughts in movement and consistent with your beliefs. When you "hear" yourself speaking scarce, fearful, limiting, judgmental or hurtful words, use that awareness as a gift to immediately change the thoughts that those words are highlighting.

If you want the "secret" Secret to manifesting your dreams, start to speak about them *as if* they're a done deal; something you already have or have had and now you're ready to accept a bigger better form. This same philosophy is applicable to the vision or intention of you being *the best you*, you can be. When the words you speak reflect your positive attitude and thought process, there is absolutely no doubt that you will become and bring everything you want to you...when the timing is right.

Your Actions and Reactions...

Every action that you take and every reaction you have to anything that has to do with you manifesting the life you envision and intend, *must* be done in the spirit of forward movement in the direction of the dreams that you've been thinking and speaking about. When you focus your actions and reactions to support your vision of getting closer to your dreams, remembering that they represent a real physical affirmation to the universe that you are very serious about this one and going to do what it takes to make it happen. Each will represent another very important stepping stone necessary to reach your focused intention. Now just watch what happens!

Whether or Not You Believe You Deserve to Have What You Want...is how you create the experience (and quality) of your life.

OK, so now you're in the game. You're spending every waking hour focusing positive thoughts on what you really, really, really want, as well as getting rid of the thoughts that are not serving you and getting in the way of your vision coming true.

You are positively speaking to yourself and others of your intentions, dreams and goals. Continuously taking right actions and making sure you are monitoring your reactions so that everything keeps you moving in the direction of your intentions, which is wonderful. BUT, if you don't believe in the depths of your heart that you deserve to have what you want, then it's all for not.

Truly believing that you deserve to have what you want empowers all your thoughts, words, actions and reactions. Because "when you really, really, really want something... all the universe will conspire in helping you achieve it.'" Really believing that you are worthy and deserve to have your heart's desire is the only way you will ever get what you want. It is a vital component in manifestation.

Beliefs are like an umbilical cord attached to your thoughts, constantly sending "blood and oxygen" to keep them alive. If the "blood" is tainted or the "oxygen" is toxic and polluted, so will be your focused thoughts as well as the end-results. You must always review and challenge your beliefs, *always* making sure that they serve your higher self. The moment there is any doubt, immediately eliminate or change them. You've got to believe that you are the best and deserve the best and expect the best if you want to realize your best dreams.

Now that you know, there can't be any reason or rhyme for you to allow any thoughts, words, actions, reactions or beliefs into your being that contradict your intentions. THE FORMULA *is the way* you create every moment of your life, unquestionably, and really vitally important that you utilize its power properly. Once you do, turning anything ordinary into your Everything Extraordinary will be *your way,* and *that way* will inspire others to be the change they want to be as well!

It all begins with a thought...

"Unless you try to do something beyond what you have already mastered, you will never grow."

Ralph Waldo Emerson

REFRAMING YOUR THOUGHTS
5th point in the FORMULA

Once you replace negative thoughts with positive ones, you'll start having positive results...it's that simple!"

In a world that is literally moving at the speed of light, there are less and less things that we have any control over. In a moment of naïveté or wishful thinking we might pretend that we do, but all it takes for a wake-up call is to see our children growing up to live their lives the way they decide to or to witness the latest congressional vote.

The list of things out of our control could easily go on ad nauseam, but that won't make any difference. What can make a difference to your moment-to-moment happiness is how you choose to process or think about any and all ankle-biting situations.

More often than not these days, I hear so many people telling me what is wrong with *life,* not necessarily their life, but *the life* they are living. So much attention is given to the people and various things that dissatisfy them on a daily basis, often under the guise of "being very selective or even discriminating, discerning, spoiled by having had or known better." The righteousness and rightness they drape over the "not settling for less or pretending that this is good enough when it's not," seems to make it permissible to allow those icky feelings of disappointment and displeasure to permeate their entire being.

When I see this happening to my friends or clients that I really adore, it almost breaks my heart. It's such a shame to see so many potentially precious moments of unbridled joy and happiness being squandered away over a chosen thought, not to mention the dis-ease and discomfort such a mindset produces within the body.

But it doesn't have to be that way. With just a few seconds of well-directed intention, anyone can readjust a negative thought into an entirely different perception that can change everything! Because of this I realized that a 5th step needs to be added to THE FORMULA; The Intention to *Reframe Your Thoughts.* Something I do 24/7 as one of my favorite go-to tools to support my highest commitment; Living a JOY-filled life.

Reframing (from Weston's dictionary), is the fine art of taking a thought, in the context of an opinion, belief or judgment that is bringing you any form of discomfort or discontent and turning it around. When you turn around a negative to the "positive reflective side" facing all the various thoughts about a situation, every sense that is activated by that thought can be *en-lightened* to serve you.

In other words, you are taking a negative thought or opinion that in some way or another is making you feel unhappy, and finding something or some way to see the same person, place, thing or circumstance from a more positive point of view.

There is no advantage in dwelling on what doesn't please you. In fact, there is a great disadvantage to our physical and mental health when we indulge in the luxury of being "a victim" of circumstances. Even though your senses are some of the few things under your control, so many people choose to use them to harm and damage themselves instead of helping or improving.

It definitely is your prerogative, but nothing for nothing, if given my druthers I sure as heck am going to find a way to encourage pleasure from all my senses. And if they're not pleasuring me, figuring out the fastest way to turn those feelings around lickety-split!

Let me give an example of how that goes.

One night my friend and I were out to dinner and we decided to go dancing at a local music spot. We both had been there many times before and we knew that this was what you would consider a C+ club. At best you just stop in for an hour at max to let loose and dance a bit before going home happy and alone after making it an early night, which is what we did.

As the clock struck the proverbial midnight and we were walking to the car, my friend began sharing all her dissatisfactions; the music was lousy, there were no good men there, the crowd is shabby, etc., etc., which clearly had affected her enjoyment of the evening. As she was speaking, it hit me how easily we could rewrite the scenario into 50 different scripts from 50 different people, all coming to the same conclusion: Someone is discontent and not happy where they are, doing what they are doing and who they are doing it with during this particular moment in their life.

Got it? I hope so, because I want to take this a step further.

This feeling that is self-created over a perceived dissatisfaction can very easily get logged into your memory bank, and all it will take to reactivate feelings of discontent, is the simplest question, or remark that has any vague reference to it or a similar situation. Eventually those feelings will morph into seemingly unrelated areas and without you even realizing it, you will spend much of your lifetime burping up the gaseous remains of toxic thoughts and memories.

I was first introduced to the gift of *Reframing* by my friend Joanne, a fabulous woman who has surmounted her share of ups and downs. After years of studying with master teachers, she has come out on the other side as a joyous, confident risk-taker. As a strong proponent for never stopping to move in the direction of your dreams, especially when there is no proof that you will even find what you hoped for once you got there, *Reframing Your Thoughts* is advice which has served me well.

"*Reframe,* reassess, reposition, repurpose and rethink the way you see and think about *whatever* isn't bringing you inner peace and joy. If you see that your opinions or beliefs about something are making you feel less than joyful or happy, *Reframe* those thoughts in such a way that this exact event can now be seen in a positive self-serving way.

It doesn't matter if those negative perceptions or thoughts are *Reframed* into some sort of yet to be proven fantasy, all that matters is that you are always filled with positive bubbling emotions. That way the parasite of negativity can't ever settle down and get comfortable inside your being!

There is no win in focusing on what you are not capable of changing that is not to your liking, such as the people or environment that you happen to be with at that moment. Unless it's possible to say sayonara or do something about it, as mentioned above, the best thing you can do for yourself is find the rainbow in the cloud, the gift you know you will discover later. Right now, find another way of seeing and thinking about what's going on, so that you can feel joy where you are."

Reframing your perception about a person or an experience can completely change the dynamics, and you will be amazed at the transformation in the quality of your life once you do. It may take a little work and a few re-dos's, especially if this is a new concept to you or the experience is particularly difficult or painful. But once you fully embrace the concept that every single event can be seen from many different points of view, and how you choose to view everyone and everything is what determines your state of mind and physical health, the quality of your life will dramatically change for the better.

I was at the same C+ club as my friend, but I chose to *reframe* my thoughts to be in a state of gratitude that it was a nice breezy night for dancing outside at a club just down the street from where we had dined. The band was playing some great songs to dance to, I got to see a few friends, and for me, the other people just filled out the club as if hired extras in my own on-going novella. Once I had enough and was equally content to call it a night I went home after having a great time, as I always fully intend to do when I go anywhere.

I've learned that it is our perception, point of view, opinions and beliefs that create our philosophy and mind-set that ultimately will design and define the experiences and quality of our lives. You must always, continuously, examine your thoughts and always stay consciously aware of not regurgitating any ideas that can activate feelings of discontent. *Reframing* your thoughts so that they up your vibrations, while staying vigilant to removing thoughts that deplete your positive energy, is the perfect 5th point for The Formula for The Art of Living Well!

The actual circumstances of your life matter less to your happiness than the sense of control you have over the way you think and feel about the circumstances of your life.

When you use the ability to *Reframe* the way you interpret the moments of your life so they always bring you joy and happiness, you will become a master at creating The Best Life Ever!

En-JOY!

Find yourself and express yourself in your own particular way. Express your love openly. Life is nothing but a dream, and if you create your life with love, your dream becomes a masterpiece of art.

Don Miguel Ruiz

How to be a
MASTER OF CREATION!

"The word is a force you cannot see, but you can see the manifestation of that force, the expression of the word, which is your own life."

Don Miguel Ruiz

Ponder these questioning thoughts...

What would it take for the little chickadee called *you* to hop off your soft smooth protected ledge into the free-fall of life? What trepidations, colossal fears, huge challenge or massive obstacles would you have to overcome to ease off of this supposedly safe space and dive into the unknown? What could possibly be the catalyst that ultimately empowers and eventually give you the necessary courage to step out of your comfort zone, (which as we all know in the depths of our hearts is not at all that comfortable just familiar),to finally realize the life you so desire?

Interesting thoughts to ponder, don't you agree? Now ask yourself the mother question of them all; What beliefs do you have that could be holding you back from having the Extraordinary life you truly desire and know you deserve?

When those questions were first posed to me, my first inherited response was to not fully own any of the fears or beliefs that were limiting me. But the more I stayed with the challenge of honestly answering all these questions I was forced to admit that there were certain aspirations I had yet to realize. The idea that I was the one responsible for not creating the life I've envisioned, because of beliefs and concepts I had developed and was now using as the reason for what I have or do not have, was quite upsetting.

As the expression goes, "When the student is ready the teacher will appear," and *this teacher* is often in the student mode. I've learned to live with an open heart and a willingness to receive still yet another life lesson that could improve my life from whomever, whatever and wherever it might come.

Beautiful Ellie walked into my life at a lovely garden party, coincidentally just weeks after she had received a birthday present of *How an Ordinary Woman Can Have an Extraordinary Life*. She stepped into a spirited discussion I was having with a mutual friend. When she suddenly looked at me and her eyes went really big as she shouted out in glee, "It's you! The joy-filled woman who is teaching us all to turn our ordinary life into an Extraordinary one: You are truly a *Master of Creation!*"

Master of Creation: What? Who Me?

"Absolutely you are a *Master of Creation!*" she said. "The concept of *The Formula* you are sharing is so brilliant! The message of focusing on using each step of

The Formula with a commitment to get positive results is exactly how a master creates! What's so cool is that once each and every person gets it, we potentially could solve many of the world's problems besides our own!"

Ellie went on to say, "As you stated, whether this power is used positively or negatively will determine the results you get and the quality of your life. If you chose to create your life by following the steps of The Formula with a negative mentality, consciously or unconsciously, without doubt you will get negative results. You will still be a Master of Creation, just not a very good master of effectively using your innate powers."

Wow, this was the first time anyone had such a perfect interpretation to exactly what my Formula "discovery" was all about! Her reiteration of my epiphany made me understand it at a much deeper level than even I had realized, and now that all the circumstances of my life had been so dramatically changed, (my long time marriage ended), I was now obligated to *walk my talk.*

My world as I had known it had been turned upside down and I metaphorically felt as if "I had been tossed off the Lily-pad, thrown into the murky dark waters and forced to come onto the shore naked." *Dripping wet,* I went to my daughter's beach condo to heal and regroup.

I cried on and off for days, took beach walks while communing with God, soaked in at least six salt baths a day, and in between tried to read books and listen to CD's that would help lift my spirits. I've created many

things in my life that I am very proud of, but it had
been a long time since I had to create a completely new
Extraordinary life totally for myself, and admittedly,
I was scared and not so sure I could really do it.

During one of my beach jaunts I heard that voice in
my head again saying, *"Joy, my love, I know you are
not pleased with the way I pushed you out into this new
adventure, but enough was enough. I sent you 'various
messengers' but you chose not to listen to the warnings.
What else could I do?"*

So this "new adventure" that I certainly did not design
or plan on, was the way the universe decided to get my
attention so I could do what I needed to do to be all the
woman I needed to be. By pushing this little chickadee
off her smooth, but not so smooth, safe, but not so safe,
comfort space, I had no choice but to fulfill my destiny
to become a totally self-reliant joy-filled woman as *a
Master of Creation.*

You see in one form or another, I felt as if I always had
some sort of a safety net under me, which I must admit
I found that thought very comforting. It began with my
loving, supportive extended family, and has continued
through all my relationships with family, friends, lovers,
husbands, life and career experiences. Like everyone
else I have had my share of pain, suffering, betrayals
and disappointments, but even as a little girl I had a
half-full mentality and knew that I was one of God's
blessed children. Unconsciously, I expected everything
to always stay the same.

Whether this safety net theory was really true or not doesn't really matter. It was *my belief* and it certainly had a lot to do with my joy-filled state of being. But in retrospect, I saw that it also had a negative effect on my self-confidence in believing I could be totally self-reliant if push came to shove.

There was always that annoying little unexamined piece of whether or not I would really be that "fabulous, magical, dauntless, omnipotent and goddess-like" when left to my own devices, to not just simply survive, but to flourish in the real world. Well, the silver gauntlet had been thrown down and I knew that the time had come to see what his *master* could ultimately create.

Sounds strange, doesn't it, coming from a fairly attractive, fairly successful, fairly confident woman? Well, guess what darlings, inside lots and lots of fairly attractive, fairly successful, fairly confident women, at one time or another, is a little girl afraid of who or what she will find in that dark scary closet of the unknown.

Staying with the little birdie analogy, when I was nudged out of the safe and protected middle of the V formation, I had no other choice but to assume the lead position and to figure out how to navigate through the previously undisturbed air to finally at last become all the woman I was meant to be.

The burning question became: "*If Not Now, When? If Not You, Then Who?*"

What I have learned through a conscious practice is that once you fully embrace and acknowledge your own responsibility for the outcome of the life you are now living, as well as for the intention of how your future will unfold, all sorts of unexpected wonderful exponential results occur. Add to the affirmation of being *A Master of Creation* the words *"I am"* and you have affirmed The Source connection to the end-result, which is absolutely unstoppable.

Taking ownership of all that comes with saying *I am A Master of Creation* is really a very powerful affirmation. It declares to the universe that the jig is up and you are no longer giving credit or blame to anyone else but *You* for this experience called *Your Life*. When you look back over the peak events of your life and proudly claim full rights, with equal if not more time than you spend on remembering your failures and disappointments, that realization alone is totally empowering.

As I've said before, the actual circumstances of your life matter less to your happiness than the sense of control you have over the way you think and feel about the numerous and varied circumstances of your life. When you have the ability to return to your peak experiences and the personal power it took to achieve those results, the action Abraham Maslow says all truly successful actualized human beings do, you will have become a *Master Of* (the) *Creation* of living Your Best Life Ever!

You cannot change the parents who birthed you or the things that have happened in the past. You can't change the way people act and rarely the ultimate outcome of events. But you can change how you *choose to view* the outcome of all the various circumstances of your life.

I believe that if we ask for something we want, that God has only three possible answers to any of our requests: "*Yes...Yes, but not right now...or...No, because I have some- thing better in store for you.*"

Acknowledging that you are a connected to a loving generous Source, and as a *Master of Creation* the one responsible for the quality of the life you are now living~ which includes the good, the bad and the in-between~ can be very exciting, especially when you to understand that it puts you in control of your own destiny!

So, go fly my little chickadees and chickadudes, as high and as far as you desire. The weather report says beautiful clear blue skies, few clouds and no foreseen insurmountable obstacles. Just stay away from the shiny spinning things.

En-JOY!

"Flow with whatever may happen and let your mind be free. Stay centered by accepting whatever you are doing. This is the ultimate!

Chuang Tzu

MY FAV THREE "go to's"...
to stay centered and on course

"There is no affirmation without the one who affirms ~ in this sense, everything to which you grant your love is yours."
                                                    Ayn Rand

As hard as it is for me to believe, it has now been more than 25 years since I was abruptly awakened at some ungodly hour with this wild premonition that, once realized, changed my entire life forever. A premonition, which came from a "dream" predicting what my future was going to look like within the next five years; most importantly, *that I would know that I know.* That I would finally understand so many of the mysteries of life that I had been seeking for decades, as well as how to utilize this knowledge that would totally transform my ordinary life into a truly Extraordinary one.

This epiphany became the foundation for the book *How an Ordinary Woman Can Have an Extraordinary Life: The Formula for the Art of Living Well* that was designed to give result-oriented solutions to many of the issues that had limited me for years, specifically issues that had hampered my personal growth.

I felt fairly safe in assuming that these same concerns had limited many other women, and that they might want the answers as well. Obviously I was correct, since that book went on to be a Best Seller in many countries.

"They say" that when you are in the flow of what you are meant to be doing all sorts of gifts in all sorts of different wonderful ways will be delivered to your door. Great ideas, people, opportunities and challenges, all designed and orchestrated just so you can realize your most desired intentions. For me, it's to be The Source of Life showing up as JOY!

With this intention as my guiding light, I always try to practice what I preach by refining and perfecting my theories, and continuously seeking out different ways to up my game, while trying to embody the role-model persona I have admired in others. With that in mind I now am going to share my **FAV Three** *"Go To's"* that I use when I am feeling frustrated, a bit lost or fearful, and need to return to my center and back on my course.

1. "Are You In or Are You Out?"

Somewhere along this journey called "My Life," I must have picked up the notion that affirmations~ statements that you declare to be true~ actually work. Because clearly unbeknownst to my conscious awareness, I have been using them for a really long time. My main one I repeatedly use when good and bad things happen to me that are definitely *not* expected, invited or welcomed, and for sure, not part of what I think is my perfect plan.

Something that have me saying to myself, "Joy, you may not see the gift in this person or situation at the moment, but trust me; *Everything has a reason for being... Everything always works out in your favor... because you are blessed.*"

I can't even imagine how many times I must have repeated these words in all sorts of circumstances; uncountable. But what I can tell you is that I believe these words to be true, and that belief brings me peace. It's like seeing the rainbow hidden behind the dark clouds while you're still in the storm. Sooner or later, you know everything will work out fine, so why not just relax and enjoy the light show?

But an affirmation in any form only works if it is your truth. So when I had decided to go listen to my friend singing at a new club I'd never been to before, I did get directions, but honestly I half listened to, since I "was sure" I knew exactly where it was. Wrong. I got so lost it was ridiculous.

I purposely wanted to go early and go alone, since Sam often brought me into his act, so to speak, by playing off of me with his great repertoire of 50's and 60's music, which we both enjoy so much.

So as each wrong turn I made turned into another wrong turn in a neighborhood I had never seen before, my happy "joyous" mood started to get gray, definitely heading towards black. It was getting later by the minute and getting lost in this dark foreign area was definitely bringing out the worst in me.

My negative attitude did not go unnoticed. The idea that I was letting myself go there and feeling incapable of reframing my thoughts was equally upsetting~ so much for "walking my talk."

Then out of nowhere. I heard "that voice" say, *"Are You In or Are You Out?*

What? What the heck does that mean, *"Are You In or Are You Out?"*

"You heard me right Joy, Are You In or Are You Out?

Do you believe in the affirmation you have repeated hundreds of times, that Everything has a reason for being...Everything always works out in your favor...and that you are blessed?

Because If You Do, then your being lost has "A reason for being, and Everything will work out in your favor... because You are Blessed!"

Well I'll be darn. How was that for being called out on my stuff! Either I faced the reality that I have been a major *BS'er* for most of my life *or* I had to own and believe these words that I have been saying for so many years. So the question really is, *Are You In or Are You Out?* You either believe your words to be the absolute truth or you don't; it's your call.

"Are You In or Are You Out?" is an amazing question to ask yourself when you see that you are going directly against what you have been saying is your truth! This was such a huge epiphany. I barely could stop talking

about it once I got to the club~ which I finally found by googling my friend's name and the club's address came right up!

To wrap this story up in a pretty "reason for being" ribbon, I arrived at the club just as my friend was starting to sing a song we always played with together, called *Hit the Road Jack.* So I just sauntered up to him on the dance floor and started lip-singing the female part, much to his delight as well as the entire audience. It was truly a JOY-filled moment had by all!

If I had arrived a mere five minutes earlier and had been seated, it wouldn't have had the same effect as me seemingly coming out of nowhere or been half as much fun! So now whenever I get upset about anything, I say my imbedded affirmation now cement with the perfect question. *Are you In or Are You Out?* It works every time to get me centered and back on course.

2. Using Created Rituals to Cement Your Affirmations...

So now that you all know that I do believe in using various forms of affirmations to empower and realize your dreams, and clearly I believe in using them a lot. Whether they are pictures or statements pasted on a vision board or words you speak or read frequently doesn't matter. *Affirming* is the reinforcement that is the glue to cementing a vision, dream or goal.

But that being said, I've never have been a proponent of repeating positive statements that in your heart you don't truly believe to be true. "I am thin" (when you you're twenty pounds overweight) "I am wealthy" (when you don't have rent money) "I am healthy" (when you are coughing through your second pack of cigarettes.). Unless you really believe what you say, your negative self-doubts will override all your hard work because they are not your real truth.

But what I do believe works is creating many varied *Affirming Rituals* that reinforce what you fully believe and intend to be your truth.

For example, I personally really am striving to be considered an 'ageless beauty," which gets a bit more challenging as I am granted another glorious year on this incredible planet called Earth. With that said, it makes me more determined to do what I need to do to have what I really want, such as being a healthy fine example of a youthful spirit and body.

So each morning I begin my day with a *healthy* green, antioxidants and almond milk shake, just to *affirm* my desire to keep my body well-fed before I begin any of my mentally and physically exercise. As well as staying fit and trim, feeling connected spiritually has always been high on my priority list. So by taking that extra effort to get in the car and drive to the beach every day and then walking for over an hour "communing with God," totally covered with sunscreen and an extremely large hat to protect my skin, *affirms* my commitment to align with my spirit while protecting and maintaining my natural gifts... as well as helping me to finally create the sexy booty I have always wanted! (Which are words I actually have on my vision board!)

This realization was monumental for me. Once I saw that creating rituals that *affirm* what you say you want and who you say you want to be are so powerful, I have gone on to develop different ones in almost every part of my life. I absolutely believe that by *affirming* to yourself that repeated right actions will bring you closer to what you want, and staying with them day after day, is a huge affirmation to the universe that you are serious about this one and welcome with appreciation and gratitude all the help you will get along the way!

3. Listening to Your Body....

I have also always believed that your body was created to be able to heal itself, and that it "speaks" to you in many different ways. It always let's us know what is going on inside our minds and bodies, sending little hints and directions as to what is needed to keep you healthy in all areas of your life. For sure, to make the mind, body and spirit work in perfect union is definitely a challenging opportunity. But if you take the time to *listen to your body* and what you are being told... your work is to just *answer the call.*

In the process of using all the tools I have just shared with you and seemingly doing all the right things, I still had a real scare the other day. I was taking my normal beach walk when suddenly I felt this serious tightness in my chest. It was the kind of tightness "they say" could be a signal of a serious heart attack, except I somehow intuitively knew that wasn't the problem. So I went to my favorite source for the answer to everything, Google, and found a post from a runner who had the same issue. He said that if he stopped for say five minutes, when he began again it went away. It sounded good, so I tried it.

Well that worked for a while, but then I started to notice that this tightness was coming on in all sorts of various situations and different times of the day and night. I still intuitively knew it was something else, so once again I returned to "my source: to find my answer. This time what I found resonated as correct; I had and was having what turned out to be mini-anxiety attacks. Once I analyzed this signal my body was sending me, I realized it for me to be aware that I was having some sort of negative response to a negative mental thought.

At first it was a bit alarming, but then I saw what a real gift this was! Seriously, stop and think about how cool this is. My body is sending me signals to let me know that for whatever reason I am thinking negative thoughts that can potentially put toxins into my body that could lead to major dis-ease. These mini-anxiety attacks that were momentarily uncomfortable were so that I could *answer the call* and do something about it before it really became a problem!

I immediately did what felt like right action and the proper reaction, and started to research all I could on the subject. What I discovered was that these feelings are exacerbated by some sort of fear created from any sort of negative thought; big or little, silly or serious.

For example, it began with a silly sort of "fear" that strangers on the beach were all thinking that the new beach hat I was wearing, was ridiculously big. Or the next course, I wasn't even giving for another month, won't be a huge success and that I am going to not be at some "not to be miss" great event and never to be invited again, because I have been locked away writing! Silly as these thoughts may seem, and you all have had similar ones, in our mind and body they seem serious.

Thanks to this amazing gift, I now could *listen to the call* first by asking myself the right questions. Such as, "do you know this fear to be true? Are you sure you know this to be true?" "Do you have any proof that your fears will come to fruition? Absolute Proof?" Because if not, let it go. All is perfect in the world.

The tightness in my chest was just another way of the universe reminding me of my number one FAV, either *You are In or You are Out.* Either I trust that God is always on my case and all things are always happening and going according to schedule, and all I need to do is to just *relax and trust* and remember that "*Everything has a reason for being~ Everything always works out in my favor~ and I am blessed.*"

There was no need for me to be worried or anxious about anything, certainly not what strangers may or may not be thinking, (for the record, at least six people came up and told me that they loved my hat and my events were a huge success!). *En-JOY!*

"I can control my destiny, but not my fate. Destiny means there are many opportunities to turn right or left, but fate is a one-way street. I believe we all have the choice as to whether we fulfill our destiny, but our fate is sealed." Paulo Coelho

FIND YOUR LIFE PURPOSE...
~ *With* "JOY's" *inspired* *How to's!* ~

"Living in a way that reflects one's values is not just about what you do...it is also about how you do things!"

   Have you ever felt like a beautiful carousel just going round and round day after day with the same painted thoughts: Why am I here and what should I be doing with my life? Pontificating, ruminating and doing all sorts of other 15-cent words in the pursuit of unearthing the one definitive answer to *The* BIG *Question:* How do I *find my Life's Purpose?* Me too!

   I've climbed mountains, crossed oceans and sat twisted like a pretzel at the feet of many revered and respected sages for hours. I've read, listened and participated for days on end, puzzling over whether I was on the wrong path or if I'd ever find an answer at all! Until one uneventful day I suddenly realized that I had forgotten that I have known that answer forever; Thanks to the God-sent enlightened beautiful mentor in Apartment 23B.

Goldie, my utterly charming upstairs neighbor in Society Hill, became my "life coach" when I was just a young bride. Even in her advanced age she was still one-hell-of-a broad, and that's putting it mildly. As a well-educated woman with great style and grace, she would design well attended soirees in her home that to this day have created lasting friendships with many notable new thinkers who encouraged her liberal and tolerant mind-set about almost everything.

I always looked forward to and treasured this special time we spent together, especially when she would enthrall me with tales of her life laced with pearls of wisdom. One of the most memorable was on how to find your Life's Purpose while staying shapely, which she believed were solved the same way!

"You have a special gift," she would say, "and it was never meant to be such a mystery or so difficult to find. It's your destiny nestled in your heart just waiting to be claimed. In fact in so many little ways, you are already living it.

Whether faced with insurmountable obstacles or overwhelming success, your core Life Purpose is the same as everyone else's. If you follow your Joy, no pun intended, and stay the course, your calling and unique gift will naturally reveal itself. There is no one path that is better than another. What and how you choose to do what you do is up to you.

Life is an amazing adventure meant to be loved, appreciated and fully enjoyed. When you make that your calling, you will have found *Your Life Purpose!*"

Can't wait another minute to figure out how? Then jump right in and begin this minute to practice dear Goldie's *"JOY" inspired how to's.*"

BE HAPPY, KNOW True JOY...and make sure you LOVE ENOUGH!

This number one *"how to"* says it all. The Source of it all wants from all children to *Be Happy, Know true JOY* and to *Love Enough.* When you are engaging in some aspect of these various emotions and fully embracing and sharing them with others, you are living your *Life Purpose!* If this answer seems too simplistic because your life is very difficult or has many challenges, think of a time when your prayers were answered and the many blessings you have received. I will bet that feelings of Love, Joy and Happiness were part of the gift.

Sometimes to feel happy, JOYful and loved might take reframing a thought, acting *As If* or *Faking It Till You Make It.* Whatever it takes, Just Do It! Focus on "the gifts" that come with the answered prayer, because it is in that space of appreciation and gratitude that you will find all your answers.

Joy Inspired Tip #1: Want to know if you're living your Life's Purpose? **Ask yourself** *"Am I having fun yet?"*

When you take on the "Do Whatever" Attitude to *Be Happy, know True JOY* and *to Love Enough,* all of life's mysteries will reveal themselves to you. When you are happy and enjoying the process as much as you love the results, you will joyfully do whatever it takes to do and get what you want. Miraculously and magically everything seems to fall into place.

DISCOVER WHAT JUST *YOU* WERE CREATED TO DO JUST *YOUR* WAY!

No matter how important or financially successful your talents have made you, even the best are only the vehicle; in fact, maybe just one of many vehicles to *Finding Your Life's Purpose.* Your real job is to discover your special unique way of expressing what *Only You* were created to do and then do it. When you honor the difference you make that positively affects the world, you will not only realize your special calling and Life Purpose, but have the joy of living it!

Joy Inspired Tip #2: **Stop ~ Look ~ Listen!**

At different times on different days, *Stop* and notice what you are feeling. Are you feeling frustrated, angry, impatient, or passionate and enthusiastic? *Look* at what you are doing. What part of what you are doing brings you pleasure and makes you feel happy? *Listen* carefully to the whispered answers of your heart as they speak your truth. When you can happily do the work that you need to do to get what you want, and then lovingly share the process, the cause and effect will help motivate and inspire you as well as others.

DARE TO DREAM ... EVEN BIGGER!

To be that someone who is determined to follow their calling and visions you need to be a fearless spirit who dares to dream. It will demand the strength of belief that provides the courage to knock on yet another door, to trust the unknown, to have certainty right in the middle of uncertainty--especially when you have no proof of the outcome--that kind of thinking creates a life of magic and miracles. It's inevitable.

Joy Inspired Tip #3: **Dare to reach for that Heart held dream just out of sight.**

When you dare to reach for a distant impossible possible dream, you open your mind and heart to the energetic flow of perfect order and unlimited resources. Happily, you do whatever is necessary to joyfully take better care of yourself, which makes you a better, more loving, healthier, giving and caring human being. If you have a desire, the will power and passion to live your life on purpose, everything will fall into place.

TAKE ACTION.... NOW!

On the road to discovering your special gift there are many different signposts, each suggesting the right direction to go. Sometimes your decisions are spot on and everything works out hunky-dory... and sometimes they're not. But *sometimes* that wasted effort, that poor choice or huge mistake, turns out to be exactly what you needed to do. That's why you must never stop taking action, moving forward and working on yourself, because you just never know. Life is filled with twists and turns, a maze of stops and starts that all lead back to your beginning. It ain't over till it's over, and it ain't over till you are on the other side.

Joy Inspired Tip #4: **Always, Keep moving in the direction of your dreams**.

The Source of it all has a plan for you and me, and we all have a definite destiny; unfortunately, we aren't privy to either. So the best you can do is take action, one foot in front of the other, keeping your intentions focused on the dream of who you want to be and what you want to do.

That could mean just sitting down and doing the work or possibly just getting out of your own way by simply stepping aside. You might not see it, but trust me on this one, the universe is always working on your behalf. Just *Be Happy... Know JOY... Love Enough...Dare to Dream Bigger...* and *Take Action, Now.*

BECOME WHO YOU ADMIRE THE MOST...

As Like attracts Like, so do strongly held intentions. If your intention is to realize your unique gift and use it for a greater purpose, I strongly suggest finding someone you greatly admire who is using their power for good and pattern yourself after them.

Anwar Sadat, the president of Egypt, an advocate for peace and equality between all people, once said these words that really helped to change my life. He said, *"There are no extraordinary people, just ordinary people who are extraordinary thinkers."* If you then study the way someone you admire thinks and acts, and then adopt their behavior to what is within your comfort zone, you will become Extraordinary in your own special way."

Joy Inspired Tip #5: **Seek and you shall find**.

Even when you get it, are willing to dare to dream, take the necessary action to discover your special gift and then use your talents or success to enhance others, sometimes you are left feeling as if something is still missing. As my memoirs prove, I have found that by seeking out examples of those who have lived a part of their life as you wish for yourself, you can find many role models to emulate and guide you to your wildest dreams.

Living Your Life Purpose and creating a particular body part that is more to your liking all goes back to *Tip#1: Be Happy, Know Joy, and make sure you Love Enough!* Become your best version of who you admire the most by taking the right action of daring to dream to discover what you were designed to do, and you will be living Your Life Purpose! Now go put a little Gold(ie) in your pockets and... *En-JOY!*

"Why not seize the pleasure at once, how often is happiness destroyed by preparation, foolish preparations."

Jane Austen

HAPPINESS ~ PLEASURE and All That Jazz...

"The noblest pleasure is the joy of understanding." Leonardo da Vinci

It's true; I am in the JOY business...not the pleasure business. I absolutely do believe that JOY is one of the greatest of human emotions that anyone can experience, much deeper than *Pleasure* and way beyond *Happiness*. *But* without those happy feelings and varied delicious moments of pleasure, there would be no JOY! It's sort of like the question, "which came first, the chicken or the egg?" So I ask you, which came first, "the emotion JOY or feelings of happiness and moments of pleasure?" Who can ever say, since you can't have one without the other!

Years ago I had the pleasure of meet this fascinating woman from Budapest, Julia was her name, and she was for sure the closest to being a hedonist as anyone I've ever met. The main reason I could never give her that "full title," is because a real hedonist values pleasure above anything else. As much as Julia was definitely a devotee of having pleasure, making a difference in the world *while she is having pleasure* is how her value system worked, and I am determined to follow her lead.

"Darling," she would say. "There are never any guarantees that you will be able to do what you want, how you want, when you are finally ready to do what it is you want; Whatever IT is! Right now is the really only guaranteed time you will ever have to do what you want to do. Because that's the truth, it's your responsibility to make the most of every single moment you are lucky to have, and you really need to take pleasure seriously."

She used to say to me "always make sure that you factor pleasure into every day, just as you do with your business, your healthcare appointments, a luncheon or dinner plans." She didn't mean in the sense of blocking off some specific time, but it was more about giving yourself permission to acknowledge your worthiness to enjoy as much pleasure as possible from every moment of life.

"You need to find your bliss point, similar to fiddling with a new recipe, adding a little more of this and a little less of that, experimenting with your enjoyment buds to find the perfect balance. Once you have found out what really brings you joy, fully indulge. Just don't make the mistake of measuring your pleasure by a standard of its value or worth. No time is wasted, it all has a purpose. And don't worry yourself about having way too much pleasure, because you can't. If you did have "way too much" it would no longer be pleasurable!"

How and where you find pleasure doesn't matter, there is no competition, it's all good. All that matters is that you look for and find pleasure in whatever you do, knowing joy will be the bonus. Whether you are working at your business, painting a picture or a wall, exercising, giving back to the community, puttering in the garden, reading a book, doing absolutely nothing or writing a book; anything, anytime, anywhere, is perfect.

My favorite parable that Julia often used to reinforce her message of "pleasure is as vital for your well-being as sleep is for your mind and body at the end of an active day," began with her saying....

"To paraphrase The Talmud, one of the most beloved books of wisdom in the Jewish religion, 'when your days are done and you are standing before your creator, you won't be asked how hard or how long you worked, how much money you've earned or how much you've given away, nor will you be asked how many others you've helped or hurt along the way. Instead you will be asked, "how much happiness and pleasure have you known in your life, and if not enough, why not?" "What stopped you from fully living and enjoying the gift of life?"

To imagine that the Source that created us all will only want to know, *"Have you fully enjoyed this amazing abundant universe I have given you to live and play in? And if not...Why Not?"* Certainly should give pause for thought...and immediate action!

My *Happiness* "eye opener" came when I was just a little girl sitting in the back of my parent's car on the way to my grandmother's house. We always drove down the same streets past the same houses, same buildings same signs. So when I noticed the words on the huge black board outside of some very big white church that I didn't remember ever seeing before, I secretly believed that it must have just been erected so I could receive this important message; *Happiness is a way of life. Not a Destination.*

Wow, what a new and revolutionary idea that was! Miraculously I realized that being happy wasn't about whether I got that new shiny red bike sitting in Mister Schmitt's store window, went to summer camp in Maine with my best friend Suzie or won first prize in the art contest at school.

It really was about the moments lived in-between! I was only eight years old and not particularly religious or spiritual, but somehow I knew that the universe had sent this particular "communiqué" so that I would begin to appreciate the life I was now living, and to utilize this huge epiphany that would change my life forever.

Happiness is said to be, "A state of well-being and contentment related to Joy... a very pleasurable or satisfying experience," but unfortunately it is often translated into meaning, *"I will be really happy if...* I get the "new shiny red Porsche in Strong's showroom window," go to "the new trendy spa resort in Mexico with my best friend Nancy," or "win the most influential Joyologist award." (Did you happen to notice how similar my *wish list* is to my eight year old version?) Some things never change!

The caveat comes in the line," *I would be happy if...* I attained momentary pleasures, instant satisfaction, achievements or goals. But *Happiness*, certainly as it relates to Joy, should be more than the momentary feeling that your life is good, that you've been really lucky, realize the impossible or feel relief from some dissatisfying condition. Real Happiness is much more complex, as it includes changeability involvement with your senses and emotions. $H = S + C + V$, or "happiness equals our genetic set point plus our circumstances plus what we voluntarily change."

Happiness IS a Way of Life, Not a Destination. It can never be a final goal, but an on-going aspiration, that by its nature enhance your experience of a Joy-filled life. A quest that won't end once you have completed your bucket list, but at best will give you some direction in redefining what would bring you happiness today. *Happiness* is not determined by what's happening around you, but rather what's happening inside you.

Most people depend on others to make them happy, but *true Happiness* comes from your connection with your life. Deeply felt emotions like Joy, Love, Honestly, Kindness, and Courage are all a part of the meaning of life. When you use any of these qualities to rise to the occasion, you will become a shining example of your own strengths and virtues, a true master of your fate.

If overcoming your brain's natural tendency to use negative biases is a problem, try this exercise to turn "Your brain into Velcro for the good and Teflon for the bad, instead of the other way around."

First create a good experience. Look outside at the trees, inhale and exhale, and relax into thinking of someone or something that makes you feel really happy. *Next,* dwell on the experience for at least 10-15 seconds, while attempting to access as many of your other senses as possible; Breath in the scent of the air, feel the breeze on your face, etc. *Next,* try to think of other good things or to add those sensations to this experience. Your goal is to get as many neurons as possible firing and working together, like natural Ninja warriors!

Try to consciously absorb all these feelings, imagining that this experience is going into you like water into a sponge. They say that if you "absorb" good experiences half a dozen times a day, for as little as three minutes a day~ it will definitely change your life!

Happiness is a way of life...Not a Destination, is to remind you to seek out all of life's little treasures hidden under or behind the remains of the day. All the big and little *Pleasures* that make you happy; A hot bath on a cold night, catching up with a dear friend who you have been missing , getting the last loaf of your favorite bread for dinner, loving and being loved in return. All the big and little things, the extraordinary in the ordinary, as well as the Extraordinary anything and everything that can give you pleasure.

SO what do you think? Which came first, "the emotion JOY or feelings of *Happiness* and moments of *Pleasure?* Actually, the question should be, does it matter? Life is short...just *En-JOY!*

"I'm gonna make a change...for once in my life...it's gonna feel real good...
Gonna make a difference...
Gonna make it right...

I'm starting with the (wo)man in the mirror (Oh yeah!)
I'm asking him(her) to change his(her)ways (Better change!)

No message could have been any clearer...
If you want to make the world a better place...

Take a look at yourself and then make the change.
You gotta get it right, while you got the time... You can't close your mind!"

Lyrics from Man in the Mirror, sung by
Michael Jackson

This Too Shall Pass: How to Be a CHANGE Artist to the 10th degree

"If nothing ever changed, there would be no butterflies."

Change (so says the dictionary) is to undergo a transformation or modification, become different in a particular way or area of your life. To make the form, nature, content, future course, etc., of something (or someone) different from what it is or from what it would be if left alone."

Change, as much as we try so to avoid it, fight it, even deny it, in all its varied forms is the only constant that there is. *Everything* has a beginning and ending and takes on different forms during the process. You've been in many different kinds of relationships, and the ones you are in now are already different from when they began and will be different in just a few months. Your body today is not the body you were in just a week ago, no less 10-20-30 plus years ago. Once you accept that truth, you will begin to listen more carefully to the signals your body is always sending you for what is needed and the best way to keep your weight in check, stay in general good health and a pleasing physical appearance. Embrace the change...it's all good!

All of life must *Change* with no exceptions...it's the law. If you doubt that for a second, just look out the window at all of nature that is different in one way or another than it was just a week ago. How about those teenagers that were little babies just minutes ago or the gray haired grand mom that was once somebody's baby? Dare I mention the unknown *stranger* that greets you in the morning mirror? I think you get the idea.

Yet even though *Change* in every part of your life is an irrefutable fact, I would bet my stock portfolio that at one time or another you have blamed someone and something that has *changed* for your biggest heartache, deeply felt sadness, your greatest disappointment and despair or depression. You then try to do something about it; fix it, adjust it or amend it somehow to alter the outcome. Rarely have you viewed the *changes* for what they are; welcome guests bearing gifts that you want and need.

Beginnings are often wrapped in painful endings, yet all endings are part of the cyclical process for a new beginning. So feel comfort in knowing that there is no price to pay, or anyone judging you for staying too long or leaving too soon, not doing enough or giving too much (except your blaming self). It's all part of the process. The only thing you need to always remember when the fumes of *Change* fog your mind or pollute your good feelings is: *THIS TOO SHALL PASS.*

Emily, Emme as she likes to be called, is one of those women who felt after all the years of hard work she had finally gotten it right. She had done all the right things and now possessed all the qualities that someone should or could need to have what most of us would call a truly blessed life. In other words, in a scenario where all the t's have been crossed and the i's dotted, She felt pretty safe in saying that she'd secured her place in the happy-ever-after life of Pleasantville. So it came as a shocker when the trickster part of the universe decided to switch things up and peevishly pull the proverbial rug out from under her, deciding *on its own* that this it was time for spiritual grow and to learn yet another of life's lesson.

Emme's seemingly perfect world was turned upside down, primarily due to sustaining huge financial losses during the recession and Bernie Madoff's despicable chicanery, which then affected her marriage, some friendships and her career. Her only recourse was to start over again, with hardly anything but a slim cord attached to the belief that she could and would.

But Emme is a special woman. When anyone who heard about her great losses would say to her, "Oh Emme, I am so sorry," she would honestly reply, "Don't be. It was time for me to finally answer the call. Don't you worry, *This Too Shall Pass.*"

Answering the call is from a parable about a man who was at home when a storm began to flood his town. As the waters kept rising, various people came by to help move him to safety. First they came in a motorboat, but the man said "No thanks, God will save me," and he just went to the next floor up. Next came a plane, and his response was the same. By the time the helicopter arrived he was on the roof, still insisting that he was fine and their help wouldn't be necessary because God would be *answering his call* for help. Eventually the waters became so high they covered the entire house and he eventually drowned.

When he arrived at the gates of Heaven and came face to face with God, he angrily exclaimed, "I can't believe you let me drown. I prayed day and night, put all my faith in you, but you never answered my call and I don't understand why!"

To this God gently replied, "I did try to save you. I sent you a motor boat and then a plane and finally a helicopter! I answered your call, but you didn't respond. What else could I do?"

Emme knew that she would have to release many of her beliefs and assumptions to become a *Change Artist to the 10th degree*. But whatever it would take she was all in. Starting a new life~ which included recreating her career, making new friends as well as getting back into a very different dating scene that she had known~ would have its own unique challenges, but in her mind, *all of it* was what had to be.

As my BFF Oprah once said, *"forget about the fast lane. If you really want to fly, just harness your power to your passion."* Those brilliant words are what Emme used to fuel her forward flight through uncharted skies. Without having the large protective umbrella she had always known, she only had her desire and passion to rely to provide the momentum needed to keep going through all the trials and tribulations along the way.

Emme said that she realized that once she could replace her concerns with *curiosity*, something physical happened in her brain. "Once I expanded my limited thinking, it seemed as if I somehow opened a portal that allowed various solutions to potential negative problems to appear. It was if I had created an open space that was not corrupted by past negative experiences, therefore letting a greater intelligence operate at its full potential. Entrusting my childlike curiosity to infuse my mind and allow my intuition to lead the way, I was no longer limited by one conclusion, and bit by bit my beautiful new life began to unfold right before my eyes."

Change often takes creating something from nothing. Something or some way you never even thought about or have done before. At first it can be frightening...but it also can be quite exhilarating. Moving forward on your own terms in the direction of a new adventure or long held dream includes making choices and decisions on "this road under construction" called your life, without the need for approval or permission from anyone else.

As Ayn Rand once said, *"The question isn't who's going to let me; it's who is going to stop me!"* Having courage, conviction and confidence, matched with eternal optimism and the belief that real *Change* is possible, is a savvy secret for turning anything ordinary into Everything Extraordinary!

For sure, *CHANGE* is a mind over matter challenge, an inside job as they say. But once you are on the case, you can kick into high gear and then use every form of right action. First and foremost is accepting the fact that none of us are meant to take this amazing trip alone. In one way or another, we all need others to help manifest our visions. Being vulnerable enough to reach out and ask for help, to honestly admit that no one is a superwoman or superman, or invincible, is a very important piece of the puzzle to becoming a *Change Artist to the 10th degree.*

At the same time that you begin to create and build new relationships with family, friends and business associates, it's important to be your own counsel on solving the most fundamental mysteries of *Change.*

Ask yourself, "What exactly do I want and need to *Change*...about myself, my behavior, my attitude, my beliefs and the life I am living?" And equally important, "What don't I want to *Change* that might have been stifled or discouraged that I now want to enhance or embellish?" Be patient with yourself and the process. All the answers to these questions and ones you didn't even know to ask will be divulged as each step leads to the next.

With so many new experiences and opportunities appearing each day, taking good care of yourself is vital. No matter how involved the days gets with your other "very important stuff," affirming rituals that are sacred to you must become a high priority. Keeping your mind, body and spirit healthy and happy is so necessary for handling a life that is guaranteed to be filled with lots of *Change,* which is all of our lives at one time or another!

Yet, this is the one step that so often is ignored or at the very least put low on the priority list. When all the pressures and outside influences seem to take you over, it is your inner knowing as far as "what really matters," that will reinforce your strength and self-worth. Paying attention to your self-care is just doing what airlines have been telling us for years. "You've got to put your oxygen mask on first before trying to help another." If you are not in good shape first, you can never make a difference to anyone or anything else."

Will *Change* include having some rough spots and even some really scary moments? Absolutely! It's not possible for anyone, including greatly evolved masters, to not entertain a few moments of doubts and fears over *changes* and how they will affect the future. We are all human you know! All sorts of emotions came with your default software. But that doesn't mean that you can't control them or even deactivate the ones that no longer serve you.

Will you travel down a road or two only to find a wall seemingly too high to surmount or end up on the edge of a cliff that falls into a huge black hole? You Betcha! Will you meet along the road a new boy or girl friend, client or business associate that turns out to be "not quite the person you thought they were? Yep. But that's life. If you are going to live it, it's all a part of the journey, part of the adventure, part of the experience. Whatever it is, *This Too Shall Pass.*

It reminds me of the story about a student who went to his meditation teacher and said, "My meditation is horrible! I feel so distracted, or my legs ache, or I'm constantly falling asleep. It's just horrible!" "*It will pass*," the teacher said matter- of-fact.

A week later, the student came back to his teacher. "My meditation is wonderful! I feel so aware, so peaceful, so alive! It's just wonderful!" "*This too shall pass*," the teacher replied matter-of-factly.

Emme said she decided to make a decision to see all challenges as just another wonderful opportunity to test her innate ability to "bounce back" and quickly move to a higher better place.

"When you need to know to the depth of your soul, is that you are and have more than enough to handle *anything* that is thrown your way, by using a stick-with-it kind of fortitude and resilience, no matter how difficult or arduous things get. All things will naturally lighten up, and before you know it you are onto another much brighter side!

When you can see *Change* as the natural ebb and flow of life, then the ostensibly high wall or edge of a steep cliff becomes a gifted blessing in disguise. You will begin to see everything as another opportunity for you to step back, reevaluate and reassess what's best for you. With a clear head you can decide which direction you want to go, what gives you the kind of strength you may never have known."

Just like Emme, I didn't ask for and wasn't particular happy when my life changed so dramatically. But I have come to see that *Change* isn't a disruptive problem...but truly just the beginning of a new experience to help you fulfill your own unique destiny. When you can *change* your mind in a very deep way so that your thoughts no longer dictate your emotional state, and get to know yourself as a physical creation that at some point in time will be returned to the Source, whether you like it or not, you will *change* the way you look at things and the things you look at will *change.*

Change is the only constant. It always has been and always will be the foundation for all creation. It's perfect and you can totally rely on it. It brings the birth and death of flowers, life, relationships, bodies, habits and thoughts that haven't, but now can, positively *change* your life. Remembering that *This Too Shall Pass,* the bad and *the good,* and that everything and everyone will *change* can be quite a comforting thought! As Winston Churchill said," *To improve is to change; to be perfect is to change often."*

En-JOY!

"In my next life I want to live my life backwards. You start out dead and get that out of the way. Then you wake up in an old people's home feeling better every day. You get kicked out for being much too healthy, go collect your pension, and then when you start work, you get a gold watch and a party on your first day. You work for 40 years until you're young enough to enjoy your retirement. You party, drink alcohol, and are generally promiscuous, and then you are ready for high school. You then go to primary school, you become a kid, and you play. You have no responsibilities; you become a baby until you are born. And then you spend your last 9 months floating in luxurious spa-like conditions with central heating and room service on tap, larger quarters every day and then Voila! You finish off as an orgasm!"

Woody Allen

LUST

"Lust is an emotion or feeling of intense desire in the body, a very powerful psychological force producing intense wanting for an object, or circumstance fulfilling the emotion. While Infatuation is the state of being carried away by unreasoned passion or a desire usually inspired with an intense but short-lived passion or admiration for someone." and forever they shall be bound.

Lust, in all its glory, encompasses so much. It's hard to contain in just one thought or have any judgment about it. In some situations it can be the impetus that helps you stay the course and find the fortitude and energy to get what it is you deeply desire. Other times it can be the unwavering desire itself, as much a part of sizzling intimacy as the idea of it. Delicious and also dangerous, But as any good cook knows, when, where and how to use your spices can be exactly what will turn an ordinary meal into an Extraordinary feast.

En-JOY!

"Lust is what keeps you wanting to do it even when you have no desire to be with each other. Love is what makes you want to be with each other even when you have no desire to do it."

Judith Viorst

LUST AND INFATUATION...

"There came a time when the risk to remain tight in the bud was more painful than the risk it took to blossom."

Anais Nin

LUST; just say the word out-loud a few times and notice the feelings it arouses as it easily rolls off your tongue out into the atmosphere. To paraphrase Jane Austen, "if the warmth of the language could affect the body it might be worth reading in this weather."

LUST is an intangible emotion that causes such a fervent yearning for another that it can take over your senses with an almost uncontrollable desire called *Infatuation* that is often experienced as a Love/Hate relationship; delicious in one sense, displeasingly displeasing and bitter in another.

Lust and *Infatuation,* infatuation and lust, are so hard to separate because one is so closely attached to the other. Both include a reaction to an attraction to another person and how that makes you feel. While *Lust* tends to be short-lived, and tends mostly to be about sexual gratification in the heat of the moment, *Lust* can be heightened by an *infatuation* for this heavenly person that has you besotted and you find simply irresistible. You can't seem to help constantly thinking about the way they smile, the way he or she says your name or the way that they looked at you. You think obsessively about all sorts of details while trying to figure out how this person feels about you based on every slight and trivial action.

Lust and *Infatuation,* hand in hand takes you down a path your bemused mind can barely discern. Yet you willingly follow, because of the possibilities that could entice you. So the one big question that's repeatedly asked by men and women all over the world, is..."How can I tell if the feelings I am having for this person are because I am in love or just *Lust* or *Infatuation*?" Dr. Phil says, "There is a big difference between infatuation and falling in love. Just like there is a big difference between falling in love and being in love."

"Ain't that the truth" was Veronica's, an astute woman in my master class, response to this quote. "I've had to learn that lesson the hard way, as many of my friends have as well. Too many times my unceasing appetite for the intense pleasure I felt for another person has caused me to think that I am in love. But when the source of my infatuation turns sour or they're no longer feeling the same way, heartbreak and disappointment supersedes. Once again I am left with the feeling that love is just too difficult, too painful and precarious at best. So why even bother?"

Intellectually I know that real love isn't any of these things. In fact what I know for sure is if you have to ask "Am I in love," you're not!

"What other things have you learned from experience?" was my next question.

"Oh so much, in fact all my friends now are calling me *The Relationship Whisper!*' After my last 'Mr. Big' fling I decided to learn as much as I could about the various stages of Falling in Love~ which are *Lust, Attraction and Deep Love and Attachment.* So now if any of my girlfriends have any doubts about what's going on with their latest squeeze, we put their actions up against my 'Is it real or is it *Memorlust*' test."

"I love it! Do tell."

"Ok, let's start with *LUST,* the first stage of "falling in love" which is always driven by passionate desire and according to experts, can begin immediately and last up to two years! This stage of the romance has very specific telltale signs which are often confused with the movie and novel versions of what we take for 'real love.' It begins with a focused attention on someone that you are physically attracted to that you've now zoned in on as your new "love" interest.

If it's simply *Lust,* you will have a strong desire to have sexual relations with very little inclination to have any kind of deep emotional conversations. You want to be lovers, but not necessarily friends. In fact if given your choice, you'd much rather keep this relationship strictly on a fantasy level with no real feelings involved.

Some other clues to look for to know if you are just *Lusting* after someone, opposed to be serious about them, is to see if you're treating that person as just 'another thing' and really only interested in 'catching' them and then getting them into bed. If having any security with this person isn't important and you're only interested in how great it feels to be physical together, and after you get what you want you can take or leave them, it's *LUST*.

If you're more concerned with satisfying your sexual desires than about creating a partnership, if you find yourself getting annoyed because they might want more of a relationship, if you could care less whether you do or don't speak to them for days or weeks until you are hot to trot again; it's definitely just *LUST*."

Stage two involves *INFACTUATION*, an emotion that can really muddle things up. This "love-struck" phase is when you spend hours daydreaming about your new lover. You lose sleep or even your appetite, as all flaws and faults are blurred and a bit diffused through rose color glasses.

Dopamine, norepinephrine, and serotonin are the neuro-hormones that send your heart racing, and might actually make you feel totally out of control. These hormones play such an important role in the attraction *or infatuation* phase and once they've been let loose, all bets are off.

"So how do you know if you are Infatuated?" I asked.

"When you're *infatuated*, you are overly attracted to another person's appearance, their energy or their sexual potential. You tend to put them up on a high pedestal and aren't willing to acknowledge who they really are — good or bad. You only see them through rose-colored glasses based on who you imagine them to be. Caught up in your feelings of what you think may be love, you aren't living in reality and may even behave irrationally. *Infatuation* is an intense feeling and, in the beginnings of a romance, can be overwhelming.

Infatuation happens early on and can become obsessive. Your mind is consumed by thoughts of the other person and how much of yourself you want and are willing to reveal to this person. An idealized vision of what this person is like, which may or may not be accurate, but doesn't seem to matter at this point.

Questions as to whether you want to move the relationship forward and what this person may say about dating you exclusively may come up. If you're afraid that asking for a commitment will frighten the person away and change the dynamics, the feelings aren't deep enough yet for real love and you're probably more in the realm of *Infatuation.*"

Now just to make sure we are all still on the same page at this point, it's important to know that these feelings that are defined as *Lust and Infatuation* certainly can wreak havoc with your emotions, but they also can be a prelude to the great love of your life. The real message behind Veronica's story is not about stopping to hold onto the intention of falling madly in love with another wonderful human being. But to move forward with the knowledge and wisdom as to what your emotions are creating. To occasionally check-in to make sure you are productively moving in the direction of your dreams is a good thing.

As part of Veronica's infamous *Memorlust* test, she created this check list she highly recommends every person review if a forever love is your ultimate goal. *"Lust and Infatuation* will always be a big part of any relationship. But if your gut is telling you that you can honestly see yourself in any part of these following scenario...my suggestion is to run like hell!"

Ask yourself if...

Is there is more steam than substance?

"Love — *real love* — is about commitment and communication. These two important components are what create substance within a relationship. Of course, having the heat that comes from the steam is part of the equation, but when there's lots of drama, chaos and more gut retching blows than light and laughter, you're in a *Lustful* situation. "

Are you are more interested on the outside than the inside?

"Your first and last thoughts are always about how gorgeous this person is from head to toe, you are truly obsessed with their "big blue eyes or fabulous body" and totally enamored with their gorgeousness move than everything else, this is definitely *Lust*. When you are intentionally pushing aside any concerns about the depth and core values of this love interest just to stay in the arm candy game, then absolutely for sure *Infatuation* is leading."

Do you prefer the fantasy to the reality?

"When you pretty much know from the beginning that you don't have a future because you're similar behavior causes a level of unhealthy depravity or you are just too different and never the twain shall meet... when you know that they are never going to want you the way you want them, and they are not capable of being what you want or need... if you are letting them take you down a road that at best lets you escape from reality but is riddled with sharp objects that will eventually leave scars, it's either raw *Lust or* distorted *Infatuation* that is keeping you there."

Are you really not friends and intimacy doesn't exist?

"There was a time when you called each other the 'best of friends,' and even shared deeper truths or a piece of vulnerability. But the reality is that the desire to create the illusion of a more "meaningful relationship" was fueled by *Lust*. The intimacy that feels so satisfying and enhanced from just cuddling when you are in love, doesn't exist. "When are we going to have sex again?" makes that warm body plain annoying without it.

Are the feelings conditional at best, and you experience an intense neediness?

"Real love is about committing your heart and body to someone you love. The idea of giving those pieces to someone besides the love of your life is unforgivable. True love is unconditional, *Lust,* however, is not. Lust blurs those lines because it is steeped in gratification without other concerns.

When you can just as easily sleep with someone else and not even feel a twinge of regret, yet still have an intense need to know where and what they are doing every minute away from you to the point of even getting crazed; that is definitely a *lustful infatuation* that will cause a lot more pain than pleasure."

For sure, *Lust and Infatuation* for someone special can transform into deep romantic love, but usually it takes time. Two people can transform their *lust* into love once they have gotten to see the whole individual, including all of their strengths and weaknesses, and finally get past the 'fantasy level.'

When your focus is no longer about satisfying your ego's animal instincts with instant gratification, and you are no longer questioning how you or the other person really feels about each other, you will gain the confidence to go the distance.

En-JOY!

"There comes a moment on a journey when something sweet, something irresistible and charming as wine raised to thirsty lips, wells up in the traveler's being."

Patrick MacGill

A FRENCH WOMAN'S SECRETS FOR BEING IRRESISTIBLE

Josette always says...

"Love comes to everybody in many different ways. Attraction is always the first thing, no? But love must be more than that. It must be magic."

Madeline (name changed to protect the innocent) is one of my more "colorful" clients, and through her amazing talent to tell a story has introduced me to some fascinating characters on various topics that definitely have influenced my life. I found this particular story very enlightening and it certainly has affected the woman I've become.

Madeline (M)...

"For almost forever, boys, men, the male species in general, have always been of great interest to me for so many assorted reasons. Even when I was just a cute little kitten of a girl I liked it when the boys paid attention to me and did silly things to make me like them. This desire and feeling of control has never diminished, it just took on other forms as I grew into a rather attractive, quite coquettish young woman."

Madeline continued, "I always enjoyed the feeling of power I held over these young colts when I flirted and teased them to want me. 'CT' was what they called me, which in their mind was some sort of an insult, but because I wasn't one of those girls that 'put out,' but I took it as a compliment.
I was like honey to these young cubs, and because no one was allowed to 'have their way with me,' I became the grand prize all the fellas wanted but couldn't get.

For years that persona served me very well and I was quite content with the amount and quality of men that came in and out of my life. I possessed all the qualities necessary to attract the opposite sex, including a fit toned feminine body, shiny silky hair, a rather pretty face with green sparkling eyes and beautiful smile, or so they all said. So I never had a problem.

But recently I ended a relationship that wasn't good for me and it left me feeling a bit damaged and unsure. So last week when I met this really cute guy, I hesitated getting involved until I felt sure that I was really back on my game. To that end, I reached out for some help to my worldly wise mentor who is an absolute master in the Art of Being *Irresistible*.

Josette ,this fabulous French woman I met years ago at *The Commissary*, a cool restaurant in Philadelphia that served French food cafeteria style, which like her, was so, so chic! Josette had been an actress in various European soap operas, and as a young girl was obsessed with the idea of turning herself into a seductive siren, similar to the women she admired in the movies and had read about in her numerous erotic novels. (Personally, I always believed she fantasized about being a sought-after courtesan to some very powerful and generous man, but her moralistic background would never have permitted that.)

She spent days watching and studying their unique characteristics, and then would practice refining her talents to match. Eventually she morphed into her own version of a femme fatale with an aura of mystery and charm. She became like catnip to men, and women as well. They all envied and admired her natural sensuality and obvious confidence~ she was *Irresistible*."

Josette always said...

"If you want to be a rare jewel worthy of love and adoration you must develop a powerful ownership of your own greatness. It's a deep sense of self-esteem that originates from within and manifests as an unwavering belief in your own self-worth. Once you realize your true value and live your life from a place of high regard, others want to be in your company and will only treat you with admiration and respect."

M...

"When I first met Nicholas I immediately knew that if I wanted to be more than a fleeting fancy to this very attractive interesting man., now more than ever, I would have to rouse up Josette's fine-tuned wisdom and put the best of it into practice. The first and most important: Never Be The Pursuer.

She said that it is important that a man believe that it is his special charm and efforts that "won the contest" for his special attention. Any form of overt aggressive behavior may attract interest initially, but can greatly diminish his desire to make you no more than an interesting conquest."

Josette always said...

"The male species is a natural hunter. Always has been, always will be. The woman that truly wins the prize of his heart, among so many other contenders, has to bring a bit more to the party to stand out among the crowd. One of the most compelling ways is to use your feminine wiles is to bait and tease in such a way that makes him feel as if he is the one doing the hunting and chasing. *Mon précieux* this advice is something never to forget; after you've captured the heart of a man and even become his wife, baiting and teasing on many levels will insure you keep his interest."

M...

"I first met Nicholas at a party when he came over to say hello to our host. Within moments after our eyes met, one compliment after another came pouring out from his magnetic smile. 'I love your red dress it suits you so perfectly, and it so compliments your sparkling hazel eyes'. 'You have such a great smile, it lights up the entire room,' etc., etc., etc. Of course my smile got even bigger and I was flirtatious in a casual sort of way that said, 'Yes, I am interested ...sort of... maybe ...possibly... but very non-committal.

Giving a non-definitive response was something Josette had taught me was just the challenge hunters respond to; trying to capture your undivided attention. As always she was right, and now the chase was on.

I saw right away that Nicholas needed to see me as the *Grand Prize*, the *Big Catch* that has slipped through the fingers of less worth opponents ... but not him. Without having a PR agent standing by shouting out my praises, I needed to make sure this fella knew that I am not a one in a million kind of girl, I am a once in a lifetime kind of woman."

Josette always said...

"An alluring woman activates all the senses. First is sight: always looking your best and wear only clothes that compliment your assets. Smelling delicious is next; use your own signature scent and you will not only bring great pleasure, but become unforgettable. Sound is next; Play and tease with lots of little 'feeling messages.' Tell him 'how happy you are *feeling* this beautiful evening, how good it *feels* to be with him." Then add real feelings by casually touching his arm or hand to emphasize a fun point he has made or something amusing, then touch yourself in a seemingly unintentional way. It's all a part of The Dance of Attraction."

M...

"A touch here, a shared sensation there, different signals being sent out as to how good you feel about yourself and your life, with small brief sightings of what a life with you could possible look like. Each and every movement focused on putting Nicholas on the course to shift his energy and thoughts to staying around way past the attraction level. I like this guy and I wanted to keep his interest staying strong and then take it all the way to a real connection."

Josette always said...

"Unequivocally, nothing is more irresistible to a man or a woman than someone who is irresistible. '*Qui, pour être irrésistible, est un accomplissement digne*, to *be* irresistible is a worthy accomplishment. Much of the excitement of life is about discovering all of the many mysterious inexplicable things that are just beyond the surface, and in the attraction dance, it's the undefinable combination of your pheromones, instincts and energy that make you undeniable the *récompense supreme* (the ultimate prize)!"

M...

"Being exciting and charismatic, while still keeping my distance sexually for as long as I could, was quite the challenge. Trust me, I desperately wanted this sexy man to take me home and ravish my body, but I knew better. Despite what a lot of women think, Josette knew better when she said men do not want a woman to be so easy to get, and I definitely was following her advice.

They want to think that they are the special one to have captured *the prize,* and if you are too easy, well that certainly can put that in doubt. Besides, even when the sex is fabulous, it's a very small part of the whole story and will never win over a man's heart forever.

A woman that takes the time to understand what a man ultimately wants and needs has a much better chance at establishing a solid long-term relationship, and that takes time to develop.

Josette always said...

"A true connection of the heart has nothing to do with your intelligence, accomplishments, possessions, money background, friends or family. In fact, if you are going to depend on a connection being cemented with your logical mind, spiritual side, physical attributes or special 'talents', trust me, at best you will only create another friend, playmate, companion, or time spent with some-one who happened to be just passing through on their way to the real love of their life. The most direct way to secure a man's heart is to make him feel safe enough to explore his own feelings and emotions, and to let him know that you genuinely care."

M...

"Even though I was definitely attracted to this man, I still needed to know more about him. What he wanted, was it what I wanted? Were we on the same page? The most powerful message you can send to *anyone* is to make sure they know that the real prize is *you* and that you're not trying to convince anyone to be with you. A confident, self-assured women, or man is the most appealing."

Josette always said...

"Getting a man to be attracted to a woman is not such a big deal, it's getting him to want to keep coming back and then take it to a higher level that really counts. Learning the fine art of attracting a quality man by using the familiar skills of a 'well- trained Geisha' is definitely worth the effort. When you learn how to trigger an emotional connection through your ability to be interesting and mysterious, you become *Irresistible*."

M...

"I gave Nicholas permission that first night, and all the nights that followed, to be the man and show up as my knight in shining armor. Instead of my trying to impress him with my fascinating worldliness, I allowed him to shine. I made sure to take a moment to admire his unique and special qualities and to let him take control of how the evening was going to go. I let him be the man as I was the woman."

Josette always said...

"When a man believes that there is something special, unique and different about you, you will evoke a feeling he can't quite put his finger on it. Without the need to play any games, perform or have the perfect anything, despite the danger of losing himself, he won't be able to resist you or stay away.

You need to raise your own degree of difficulty, your status in your own eyes and downgrade his importance in your forever plan. It's a big mistake for him to feel as if you think of yourself as his exclusive girlfriend until he has fully committed to you. "

Being irresistible is certainly a wonderful and highly desirable quality, especially if you use that quality to bring happiness and joy to others. The wonderful dance of attraction has been around since the beginning of time, and Josette was a very smart woman to have learned the steps so well.

Madeline was also a very lucky woman to have been given the gift of this wisdom, as I was, post factum. I certainly hope you won't waste this generosity by not trying out a few of these moves yourself. I have, and it definitely was worth the effort. *Bonne Chance!*

En-JOY!

"I've always been attracted to women who are assertive and have confidence - qualities older women possess. They've been on the Earth a little longer. They're more seasoned. They don't play games. They know what they want, and they're not afraid to tell you."

Taye Diggs

"MAY - SEPTEMBER" ROMANCE

"The right man will love all the things about you that the wrong one was intimidated by."

There is nothing more memorable or exciting than having a vision of how you want something to turn out, and then seeing it come true. It's a confirmation that the universe is in fact listening and fully aligned with your intention to make your wish its command. Every time I have such an experience it empowers me to ask for more and reach even higher. My *May~ September Romance* was certainly one of my finest, and a piece of my life that I will remember fondly forever.

The first time I met gorgeous Garry he was working as a manager at a trendy restaurant in the Big Apple, as all actors do at one time or another. When he came over to our table, it was the most remarkable thing. Each woman in turn looked up and stopped in mid-sentence as they stared in awe at the sight of this drop dead gorgeous, truly, tall, dark and handsome man.

Once I got my breath back, my initial thought was "who do I know in the movie business that I could connect this handsome young man with?" Garry was clearly younger, 15 years my junior, so at the time I did not even entertain the idea of anything more than my helping someone with connections I might have. So I suggested he send his comp sheet to my office and let's see what I could do. See ya later alligator.

Now it's about a month later, about a week before Christmas and I am in such a deep funk. Everyone I knew, as far as I was concerned everyone in the entire city, was leaving for the holidays. All I could visualize was little ole me and dusty tumbleweeds rolling down Columbus Avenue! I certainly have done enough work on myself to know how counter-productive this line of thinking was, so I decided it was time to try communicating directly with the universe, to help me come up with a solution that would bring me unimaginable joy during this time.

So there I was walking down the street mumbling to myself, "Please dear God, help me to create something so over the top that no matter where anyone goes or what they could possibly do, won't compare to the incredible holiday I am going to have!" When who do I *literally* run into, but gorgeous Garry. After numerous apologies for knocking into him and then laughing at how nice it was to "run into" him, I casually reminded him to not forget to send me his photos before I went on my way.

By choice, I had been single for quite a while since my first husband passed away, but never considered dating a man so much younger. So when a messenger delivered the photos with a lovely card that said, "It was great to see you again, please give me a call." I decided to do just that, and to invite him to go with me to my friend's Christmas Eve dinner party. He happily accepted.

As it turned out, gorgeous Garry had only been in NYC for a little less than three months, knew hardly anyone, and was thrilled I had asked him to join me. We began the evening by getting to know each other in front of a crackling fire, which turned out to be a perfect way to begin our friendship and a marvelous evening, followed by a wonderful week spent together doing all sorts of fun romantic activities, leading up to a fabulous New Year's celebration.

I certainly have known other men, but this was an entirely new adventure. Being totally besotted by a younger man with such a sense of calm, assurance, and confidence that you would expect in a more mature man, was refreshingly different. He played with such a casual ease, only his eyes and tender touches spoke of a passion that barely contained his desire to devour me. It was madly exciting and irresistible.

When we finally did come together on New Year's Eve it was with such a passion, it left us both delirious with pleasure. Like nothing I had ever experienced before. As I looked up and beyond this truly beautiful specimen of a man to the Heavens above, I said to myself, "Thank you God...Thank you so so much!"

I wanted to have something happen to me that was so unimaginable and so spectacular that no matter what anyone else did my holiday would turn out to be the very best! Spending these fabulous days and nights basking in the attention of this outrageously beautiful man that now was my hot new boyfriend... Priceless!

From experience, I know that having the courage to break rules that by their nature are really ridiculous, such as older women shouldn't be dating younger men or they will be considered "cradle robbers," takes some special kind of strength and confidence in trusting that you know who you are and what you want.

In this crazy upside-down world, men can date and marry women multiple decades younger, and people barely comment and even suggest that it's cool. But let a woman date a much younger man and she's called a "Cougar"; a demeaning term that means a 40+ sexually aggressive woman who seeks the company of younger men. A predator in nature who is not interested in commitment, which is such a bunch of BS!

If the truth be told the women I have met who have enjoyed, loved and even married younger men are just the opposite. They are women of quality who own their power and wear it like a perfectly fitted custom-made gown. They are proud of their accomplishments and usually take much better care of their mental, physical, spiritual and financial health than women half their age!

There is no doubt that such a woman's choice of partners is always driven from what she wants, not as a conquest or what is acceptable. While younger women still use the guiles that their age affords them, a more seasoned woman comes with all sorts of extraordinary gifts accumulated over the years as part of her arsenal.

As Garry told his friend, "*She's* the catch, not the other way around!"

If every single calendar, time piece of reference or birth certificate was suddenly destroyed and no one on this earth had any idea when they were born or how young or old they were, imagine the limitations that would be eliminated.

The quality attributed to visual appearance and physical abilities of someone ten or fifteen years younger, without any surgical help, would easily be realized as there would be no reference as to how you should feel, look, act, be, etc. There would be no rules as to what you can or cannot do with whomever you want. Just imagine how life changing and freeing that would be. A wondrous dream comes true.

If you can imagine and would love to live your life in such an ageless state, and having a relationship with someone younger has always interested you, consider exploring the idea of a lover who sees no age restriction. The best compliment I received about my decision came when I overheard Garry's answer to a friend questioning him about our "*May- September*" romance.

"As far as I see it, it's up to you to weigh the pros and cons of a relationship with an older woman and decide if it is right for you. For me, let's see...the promise of mind-blowing sex with an experienced, confident, gorgeous, fascinating, classy, intelligent woman, without any games or drama or pushy expectation for a long-term commitment. Yea, I know, it's a tough call."

So if you happen to be a woman who has thought about a romance with a younger man, but haven't had the guts to act upon it because you don't know what to do, let me help you. Here are some of my best tips.

1. Retitle yourself a Sexy Kitten...

En mass, the term Cougar is used to diminish the power and attraction of fabulous mature women. It implies that anyone over 40 is prowling around hunting for their prey: the younger more innocent boy. Ha! What a joke. Especially since statistics show that it is the younger man who is seeking a more sophisticated woman in lieu of a "self- absorbed air-head, looking to be rescued, younger woman," not the other way around! So the idea of Retitling the word "Cougar" into "Sexy Kitten" is much more empowering and authentic.

2. Be Confident... Own Your Power...

When a woman owns her power...really gets her Own Magnificence...she becomes a magnet to all sorts of men, regardless of their age. Men are attracted to a confident woman who knows who she is, what she wants and what she brings to the table. A woman who no longer needs or desires to play games, has so much more to offer any man worthy of her attention.

3. Know What *YOU* Want...

It's very important to know exactly what kind of relationship you want to have with your younger man, so the experience is enjoyable and no one gets hurt or disappointed, especially since all sorts of versions are possible. Are you interested in a friend with benefits, a playmate or a committed long-term relationship? It's really important to figure this out before you even go beyond a few dates. Knowing what you both want and telling your truth, puts you both on the same page.

4. Lead with your Experience...

One of the main qualities that attract younger men to older women is that they have been around the park more than once, and tend not to get quite as emotionally involved as younger women. Because many of us have been married or have had long-term relationships and even children, we don't quickly make any assumptions or easily rush into commitments. We know that a date is just a date and not a marriage proposal. This is where your experience is most valuable; wisdom used wisely.

5. Communicate...

Good communication is premier to every kind of situation, but even more so when you are involved with someone whose differences could be a problem. Talking about your wants, need, fears, expectations and definite deal-breakers is very, very important, especially when things could possibly go beyond a love affair and lead to a much more serious relationship.

Discussing what could be differences or obstacles, such as having family together, religious or financial issues that may not mesh, etc., can help to diffuse problems that could possibly rear their ugly heads later on. Besides, seeing how your goals, dreams and desires match-up, can be very interesting and stimulating.

6. Take Good Care of Yourself...

Youthfulness definitely is an attitude. But if you really want to back up that attitude undisputedly, it helps to have a healthy mind, body and spirit. Trying your best to keep your thoughts positive, your body fit and toned and staying physically active, will help you look more youthful with a lots more energy to do the things you want with your new stud-muffin. Take good care of yourself and you'll see that age is really only a number.

Lastly and most importantly...

7. Be His Lover *Not* His Mentor or Mommy and Enjoy your differences.

It's only natural to want to share all your gifts and the knowledge you've garnered over the years, and only natural for him to want to learn things from someone more experienced. But it's those *curse it how's* that can so easily tip the balance from "loving it" to "hating it." You must never forget that you are his lover not his mother.

Often times, once "the student" believes that he has outgrown the wisdom or the need for his "mentor," the slippery slide from "that is so cool," to "I am so over getting advice," sees the passion begin to wane and the end of a great relationship right behind it.

Making the decision to date a younger man can be many things; exciting, intriguing, and an adventure into undiscovered territory. It takes a special woman to go against the norm and face the scrutiny and possible rejection of friends to be with someone much younger, or of a different race, color, religion or background. But in reality, anything we chose to do that is not within "the acceptable standard," has its challenges, as well as the potential of great rewards.

Being in a *May-September* relationship may not be for everyone, but then again, nothing is. As long as you're both happy and enjoying each other's company, and conscious of not hurting anyone, any "differences" should never be an issue. In fact, it may be just the thing to add the necessary spice to the sauce of your life!

En-JOY!

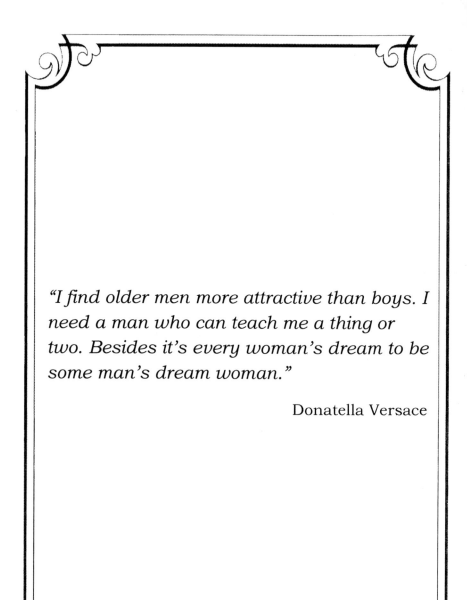

"I find older men more attractive than boys. I need a man who can teach me a thing or two. Besides it's every woman's dream to be some man's dream woman."

Donatella Versace

"JUNE – DECEMBER" ROMANCE

"Age is simply the number of years the world has enjoyed you."

Seriously, if *anything* has ever really drastically changed over the last two decades, for sure it's the dating scene. Meeting a nice guy or gal was so much easier and felt so much safer when so many of us first got into the dating game.

We would meet our prospective dates through an introduction from a friend, the family, at school, the place we worship, or at a party with friends. Someone you knew seemed to know them, and it didn't take very long before you knew everything about them that you needed to know, in order to make a fairly educated decision if you wanted to spend time with them.

But now-a-days it seems as if we are mostly meeting "strangers," thanks to the coupling game fueled by numerous on-line websites, open social gatherings or bars *where everybody knows your name,* but nothing about you. Because of the different kinds of relationship scenarios, this *unknown* factor has made it even more important to know yourself, what you want, trust your gut reactions and listen to your own inner wisdom.

With that in mind, this story is for anyone who may be considering having a serious relationship with an individual much older than themselves, which has become much more prevalent these days. Because this choice can have all sorts of positive and negative ramifications, reading another's story who has danced that dance is invaluable.

Susie is a very attractive gal in her late forties/early fifties who usually dates men around her age. Some are a bit younger, some a bit older. She never discriminates; it all comes down to attraction. So when Robert, a well-suited gentleman with salt and pepper hair approached her at an upscale restaurant bar, she was flattered and intrigued. Clearly he was *at the least* a decade older, but she found his air of self-confidence and sophistication very attractive and she wanted to know more.

After accepting his offer of a cocktail, which lead to a lovely dinner at the same restaurant, this gentleman turned out to be a witty charming conversationalist. In fact she found it quite interesting to see how much she was enjoying herself. More than she had in such a very long time. Still, the age difference, could she really deal with it? The pro's and con's began to flood her head.

"Similar to dating a much younger man, I am sure he probably doesn't listen to the same music and we're divided on what we consider the 'latest trends.' More than likely his level of physical vigor is much different than mine, forget the fact of whether he could actually be able "to perform" or not. Simply by being in different stages of our lives I am sure that his emotional needs are probably very different than mine. And then there is our own social circles including family and friends, which more than likely would bring their own challenges.

I am still in pretty good shape, and even though for his apparent age he looked really good, it is very possible that in not so many years away I could be spending hours sitting in a chair by his hospital bed, while my friends are texting me stories about their children's sports activities or their kid's baby showers!

These considerations, plus some, were dancing in Susie's head as the distinct possibility this encounter would lead to another date was becoming more of a reality. She wasn't naïve or blind to what she had seen with friends who had chosen to marry older men, but on the other hand, there were some really great perks.

"Most of the older guys my friends are involved with have it together financially and have the time to enjoy the rewards of their success, opposed to the younger bucks still fighting to get to the mountain top, spending much of their spare time in pursuit. Older men can also teach you much about life and love, offering you a very different perspective and experience from the typical dating pool.

More mature men are more open and available; after all, by a certain age they finally realize that immortality is an illusion and that they can no longer keep playing the field. Time becomes of the essence, and settling down with a good woman becomes more appealing, which is a good thing. He probably also has friends that are in serious relationships or married, and would very much like to be a part of that scene, so to speak."

So Susie decided to give it a whirl and began what became a memorable long-time relationship, and one of the most exciting times of her life.

"There is no substitute for experience, and clearly Robert has had many more years to learn from all the experiences he has accumulated. He has made most of the mistakes you can make and now sees problems coming from a mile away. He has helped, advised and guided me through various situations, that I might have had a much more difficult or painful conclusion.

In many of my relationships with guys that were my age, I always felt as if I was the teacher in one area or another. With this older man I feel as if I am actually learning more than I am teaching and that is really a nice change of pace.

Robert has had a few serious relationships and by now knows how to navigate his emotions and is not foolish or idealistic about love. He knows that commitment is work. He doesn't play games, and treats everyone in his life with great respect and integrity. Through trial and error he's learned how to treat a woman properly and be a better man in a relationship.

It's true that there are times that I would prefer going to a club and dancing the night away, opposed to having a quiet evening with a vintage bottle of Cabernet. Except for those few restless evenings, the quality of time and experiences we have together are so worth the tradeoff."

"The sex," I asked. "How does that compare?"

"Honestly, he is one of the best lovers I have ever had. He knows what he wants in bed, isn't afraid to ask for it, and also really knows how to satisfy me. He comes with years of experience in knowing how to please a woman, and he always encourages me to be free in asking and expressing myself. Many younger men are threatened if you tell them you want something done differently or infer you don't like their technique. Robert is just the opposite; his attitude is that there is no time to waste on egos in the bedroom.

In and out of bed, a more mature man who wants what you have to offer will let you know it, and mobilize to win you over. He's more attentive and knows how to be intimate. He can see that I enjoy affection in the form of compliments, shoulder rubs, kisses, etc., and sex doesn't have to always follow. After you've dated for possibly a decade or more, and had an unsuccessful marriage or two, you are both looking for a meaningful relationship. This makes the lovemaking much more special, because you know how much sincerity is behind the loving."

"And the con's?" I asked.

"As I mentioned earlier, I am very healthy and in pretty good shape, so when we have to deal with his numerous aches and pains, it definitely takes a lot for me to include it all. I also am not crazy about hanging out so much with "his buddies" and their wives who are mostly closer to his age. I sometimes feel a reverse prejudice, as if my "youth" made me less qualified to be taken seriously. He also feels that way about some of my friends, feeling like he doesn't fit in. But since we both really enjoy our alone time, we both try to limit those times on either side.

I think the biggest drawback is the feeling that one day his advanced years will creep up on him and then I will be living with another version of my grandfather, which I don't think I will be able to handle so well. But for right now, I honestly am a Happy Camper."

Susie is definitely an advocate for what's called the *June~ December Romance*, but admits that there are many things to take into consideration before you just jump in and one or the other gets hurt. First of all, she feels that it is very important that you treat each man as a distinct individual, do not generalize. No matter what anyone's age, it doesn't guarantee he's mature, nor does youth mean he's immature. She also suggests dating for at least 90 days before making any forever conclusions. "Give it a chance to get past the flurries of romance, which can often create a snowstorm you can't see past."

Another point she feels is very important to consider, is to specifically identify exactly what is making you even consider dating an older man. Is it because you desire a mature, well-seasoned partner or do you simply want a generous Sugar Daddy? Do you want a serious relationship, or is the reason for getting involved with an older man to avoid more rejection from men your own age? Or possibly could this older man you are attracted to be filling an emotional void, such as a father- daughter issue? Answering these kinds of questions honestly, can save you a lot of heartache later on and make for a stronger foundation for a lasting love.

For those of you who really want to go that route, here are a few pointers she felt would make your trip more enjoyable.

1. Get familiar with the three C's; Communication, Common Interests and Comfortable Space.

It's a willingness to take the time to always talk to each other about all sorts of things that keeps the flames burning brightly. When you each have some interest in what the other is interested in, you have things in common to talk about. When you engage in various activities together~ sports, movies, books, cultural events, travel, food and wines, it makes the conversations and the time together a lot more fun. Adding a good balance of time together and time apart, each indulging in your own interests and your own friends, will give enough comfortable space for the perfect mix, plus the added desire when together.

2. Enjoy being treated like a Queen

One of the perks of being with an older man is that most will want to pamper, even spoil you with all sorts of goodies. Get used to being treasured and enjoy seeing his profound ego-gratification from being attentive to your needs and desires. For both it's a win-win.

Just never take it for granted. We all want to be appreciated, and no one more than a man who is being appreciated and acknowledged for all his extra efforts.

3. **Always be a Woman, *not* a little girl**

I learned this one very early on from a woman who was in a successful relationship with a man much older than herself: You and he are NOT the same age, but you ARE equals. Even if he calls you "his baby" you must not act like one. Men of all ages admire women who have their own life, passionate interests and abilities. Making a man feel like your daddy/father image will get old really fast, and is the quickest way to age him and a wonderful relationship!

The bottom-line is whether you choose to dip your toes into shallow ponds or rivers that run deep, is a choice entirely up to you. Taking the time to really know yourself, what you want and need, and what and who can give you that, is all a part of creating the life you choose to live. It should always be just another option, not an obligation. So chose what works the best for you, and then just...

En-JOY!

"The purpose of life is to live it, to taste experience to the utmost, to reach out eagerly and without fear for newer and richer experience."

Eleanor Roosevelt

HOW TO PLAY THE PLAYER...

"The trick is in what one emphasizes. We either make ourselves miserable, or we make ourselves happy. The amount of work is the same."

Carlos Castaneda

I can't quite figure out exactly when things seemed to change in the man-women relationship scene, except to say that it had to have happened during the decades when I was still in "marital bliss," because I certainly never got the memo about the new rules. All I know is that at some point in time it felt as if an enormous number of females have been brain-washed and gone into agreement that if they surrender personal choices, desires and their moral code, and if they alter their natural bodies to look a certain way or become subservient to others wishes, they will get more men to want them and stick around for the long haul. When questioned as to why to acquiesce to these new guidelines, they seem to be influenced by the underlying desire and need "to stay competitive" in order to stay in the game.

Nothing for nothing, but in my observation, this kind of mind-set is definitely making it harder, not easier, for women to fully own their power and get what they really want. The moment you let someone else define your standards and what maybe considered acceptable behavior, is the moment you have forgotten who you are and the kind of life you want and deserve to live.

In this new age of courtship, a particular kind of fella has emerged whose habits are similar to the fish that are put into waters as a more natural non-chemical defense, to help eat away the scum created by overgrown killing weeds. At first they are welcome guests, as they are pretty and bring hope for a more organic ecosystem.

Unfortunately they have proven to multiply at such an alarming rate that they soon become "the scum" as they affect and take over everything that was good. In the real world this metaphor has shown up in the form of "a virus" that seems to have infected huge amounts of the male population, and avoiding one that hasn't been "infected" is almost impossible. But the encounter doesn't have to be deadly or even a problem. There is a way to use this to your advantage and even become better because of it. So with that said, let me introduce you to *The Player*.

A *Player* is a master of the art of seduction, mainly for the purpose of feeding his desire for variety, excitement and ego reinforcement. With a well-honed script that is developed over the years, he knows exactly what to say and what buttons to push that emphasizes his ability to give you exactly what you want and need. This special perfected talent is skillfully interlaced into a scenario that is equal as only found in the most romantic movies, stories and love songs.

Adoring sweet compliments are woven throughout the trappings of this new affair of the heart. Flowers, personal gifts, dining and wining at lovely intimate getaways, restaurants or music venues, special songs, repeatedly texting and sending lots of emails; all to show you how much he really cares as part of his dance of seduction. This Casanova extraordinaire, supreme sexual satisfier and master of the words of amour, he knows exactly how to entice even the savviest of the savvy. Some of the most worldly and sophisticated women have fallen under his spell, thinking that this could be a "forever more" loving relationship.

I personally know what a heady experience this can be, because unless you are one of the 1% who is still married to the same man or to God, it's more than likely that a Player has come into your life at one time or another. But no matter how good it seems to be going or how long the dance lasts, make no mistake there absolutely *always* is an expiration date with a Player.

So what's the problem? Absolutely none; unless you are one of those women who chooses to ignore all the obvious glaring signs and insists that "you have fallen in love" or believe that you are "the one" special woman who is going to miraculously make this man change his ways just for you, which he won't and can't can do, because in most cases he's a baked cake.

At one time he might have had all the qualities that are necessary to be a keeper, but trust me, that train left the station long ago.

In fact in defense of *The Player*, many will even kid themselves into thinking that they really want to and are ready to change their ways. And for a "New York minute" he believes that this time he wants to be and can be a better man, and will seriously talk about it.

Unfortunately his way of life has become a habit, and habits are hard to break. So after the passion for the chase and conquest has died down, and the Player slowly returns to the set point of who he really is, the quest for his Higher Self is shelved for another day.

Again, unfortunately, way too many women choose not to deal with this reality and prefer lingering in their made-up fantasy world. What could have been a great experience with wonderful memories turns into a regretful event with their heart being broken. This is often followed by overwhelming feelings of rejection, hurt and disappointment, and in worst case scenarios money and careers are affected and these women are left with a far greater loss; their self-esteem and self-confidence.

BUT this doesn't have to be the ending to the story, or even the story. Instead it can be a delicious tale of a woman who knows her own self-worth and values herself way too much to play games of the heart. A woman who chooses not to "pretend" anything is more or different than what it is, has mastered the ability to control her emotions and use her self-confidence to create the experience of life that she desires. In every encounter she feels like a winner and never a loser, because she knows herself and the why of her choices. In this scenario she has learned *How to Play the Player* on her terms, as it should be!

First of all let me begin by saying that these kinds of guys can bring a lot to the party and often worth the price of the admission. Besides, as the saying goes *"Someone is going to get the goodies, why not you?"* As long as you tell yourself the truth from the get-go who this fella is and where it's *not* going a savvy woman can make this chapter in her life very pleasurable!

As I said, there *definitely* is an expiration date to this kind of romance, usually around 3-4 months, when the hunt, chase and conquest phase is over, or you're over his game. Sometimes these affairs last much longer, which can be very hurtful, since often times those extra months or years are filled with lots of painful lies and heartbreaking compromises. *But* if you are the smart one and keep all of this advice in mind, you can just relax and enjoy the ride. Just keep all the Selfies and videos for yourself!

Being a mentor and communications expert for quite a few decades now, turning an ordinary life into an extraordinary one is my specialty, especially when it comes to relationships. It starts with *always* listening to your gut, especially when it's screaming *"Whoa, slow down."* When you feel the sensation to *"Stop, Look and Listen~ proceed with caution,"* Sweetheart, do it!

In any relationship, when you can *Stop* and step back a bit to *Look* at what the other person is really showing you, and then *slow down* long enough to *Listen to* what they are really saying in all the background stories when they are not trying to impress you; you will get all the clues you need to know who they are and what to do.

Living your life your way isn't about never taking risks, or being fearful about making another mistake, it's more about taking calculated risks backed with the knowledge that can help you make better choices and decisions that will best serve you.

So if you've gotten my drift and are now ready to fully enjoy the dance as well as all the perks on your terms, without investing your heart and soul where it is not deserved or pretending that "this time things will be different," great! Now I suggest that you incorporate the fine points I've listed below for having a grand ole time while becoming an expert at *How to Play the PLAYER!*

Number One....

This limited edition of romance with your Player is all about *YOU* getting what *YOU WANT and NEED* from this relationship. If a Player has zeroed in on you then he obviously likes your looks and style, so just keep on being you. Act, dress, be and do whatever pleases you. That way you will never feel as if you have sacrificed any part of you to be in the game ~which is the way I suggest you are in any relationship.

For the record, most Players prefer attractive women that are classy and not trashy, with a full life that doesn't demand his constant attention. As with most men, the more independent and desirable you are to others, the more exciting a conquest you will be to any man.

Number Two...

Fully embrace the 'goodies' your Player brings to the table, and then dig in and enjoy every bite! Don't spoil your time together focusing on his flaws. You know they exist, you know he is not *your forever*, where examining his shortcomings might actually matter. Instead put on those rose colored glasses and stash all the little things that bothers you some place out of your mind. Now you can freely indulge in his banquet of loving and savor the experience. How much fun is that?

For a woman who wants to meet an honest, quality man and have an authentic grown-up relationship, the Player's biggest flaw is that, this is not him. So there is no need to spend any time dwelling on it, because that's what makes him a Player! This kind of dude is in it for the ego boost of another conquest; never to win a prize he has to keep. And you don't want to be his keeper anyhow! Even when he makes remarks that infer "the right woman (meaning you) could change everything," never forget, these are just well-rehearsed lines from his perfected script. It doesn't make him a bad man. He is just not to be thought of as a "forever" relationship.

Number Three...

Never forget what you know to be true. This very attractive, delightful, attentive, romantic, fun-loving, generous, sexy man *is a Player*. When others insist on "trying to protect you" by telling you of his reputation, or worse, try to spin this into "this could be a real going somewhere relationship"; *Please* don't forget what you know. This guy is giving you the romance that you want and need *now,* or you wouldn't be there. Let that be enough. Save your true love and open heart for that someone special who is getting himself ready to come to you. For now, just enjoy the attention.

There is no greater power than living your life from your truth based on your inner wisdom and a conscious awareness. On the same note, if you choose to pretend that you don't know what you know, that you have no control over your emotions, or that you think you can change the unchangeable, at the end of the day you must take total responsibility for the results and your own personal development.

Number Four...

Keep yourself physically and mentally prepared for the other shoe to drop, which it will in one form or another, once his interest in the win begins to wane. Absolutely, fully enjoy every moment of the dance and all the perks for as long as it lasts, but always be ready and prepared to walk away with your heart intact. No matter how it goes down; the time will come when it's time to move on. Either he will end it in some sort of

"I am doing this for you sweetheart" fashion, or he will do something that is a deal breaker for you. However it comes down, *Do Not Take It Personally*, because you now know, a relationship with a Player *always* has an expiration date.

When the day finally does come that the reasons he was never your forever are undeniable, allow yourself to feel you're upset, pain, anger and disappointment at the fun times ending. I know it can hurt, but this is part of the process necessary for you to move on. But once you have gotten to the other side, far less damaged than so many others who "uncontrollably" gave their hearts, you will have some great stories to tell your friends!

In closing I need to say, I wrote this story not to give women a mini-tutorial on how to be moral-less alley cats, but to share some well-earned knowledge on how to be in control of your life and your own happiness. It's about recognizing that the universe sends you many different ways to experience happiness, pleasure and joy. To take the road more traveled (as in enjoying a man who certainly has been around the block a few times) while saving your heart for the right man who will honor it, is just plain smart.

As long as you are not hurting anyone and the time together serves both of you, in my mind this is exactly as it should be! It's all about not throwing the baby out with the bathwater, but loving the baby and using the water to make the garden of your life grow even more beautiful!   *En-JOY!*

"Fear, anger, jealousy, hatred of self and others are the outcomes of the lack of connectivity with your inner self. Connecting with your inner self and awakening your inner sensuality is not a luxury anymore, but it has become the necessity."

Vishwas Chavan

AUTHENTIC SENSUALITY

"Sensuality without love is a sin; love without sensuality is worse than a sin."
Jose Bergamin

Lusty, provocative, titillating, intoxicating; words that evoke a certain kind of woman that we secretly would all like to be thought of by someone at some time in our life. Not necessarily to act upon, even though that could be lovely as well, but just to know that we have the power to evoke such powerful emotions.

This God-given ability to arouse such interest in the opposite sex was imprinted in the female DNA at her conception of life, and it's apparent in every species on the planet. For many, this inborn talent is greatly misunderstood, drastically under used or downplayed entirely, which is such a shame since this gift is not to be wasted. Luckily, some worldly-wise women have awakened me to the power of my female energy, so now as a worldly-wise woman myself I happily passing that gift on to you.

I first fell in love with the word *"ripe"* in relation to my womanhood when some years back a certain special gentleman admirer likened my persona to *"a luscious piece of ripe fruit."* The visual of a ripe juicy peach at its perfection, firm and rosy yet succulent to the taste, seemed like a wonderful way to be viewed...similar to a J.Lo or Sofia Vergara version of womanliness, which I have always greatly admired.

These women embrace their femininity completely and are unabashedly sensual in almost everything they do, yet rarely are they sexually frivolous. Because of that distinction, they have had many men love them, take care of them and marry them, while never letting anything deter them from developing their mind, talents or their sense of love, joy and spirituality ~ The source of *Authentic Sensuality*.

Authentic Sensuality, in essence, comes from how tuned in you are to your feelings and how invested you are in experiencing all the delights of the senses.

The smell that is emitted from the bouquet of the unknown, the sweet taste of something yet to come, the clear sight of a new possibility, the sound of a whispered calling and the touch that feels new and exciting, are all a part of the journey to living a joy-filled life. "Sensuality likes to make love at the border where time and space change places," and with an adventurous spirit that is not particularly quiet, your sensuous body movements can reflect your aliveness in so many delicious ways.

A ripe sensual woman is a confident woman who fully inhabits her body. She has learned to treasure all the curves and delights of her temple and has taken the time to get to know and enhance all her attributes; whether they are well defined arms, the sway of her hips or the contour of her back. Maybe it's the swell of her breasts, the roundness of her buttocks, the slimness of her ankles or possibly the strength in her firm strong legs. Whatever her body type or structure she loves it, and that includes all the bits and pieces that she may not see as her "best attributes," simply because it's her body.

This kind of woman understands her unique style and is comfortable in expressing it. She has learned how to cultivate her subtleties and intricacies. It may be her alluring "come hither" voice, in and out of bed, the mischievous twinkle in her eyes, or her beautiful mouth enhanced with her magnetic smile. Attributes refined with years of experience and a well-developed mind.

A "well developed mind" gives you the strength to relax around what used to cause angst and pain and the good opinions of others.

Self-belief is the backbone of sensuality and the beginning of independence. When a woman decides to take full responsibility for her decisions and trusts she can handle almost anything, being independent and authentic in every sense of the word, is her only choice.

What makes a woman independent is her desire to become the *Shero* in her own story and the master of her fate. It has nothing to do with "the reality" others see, only what she chooses to see and act upon. Limited only by imagination, she never considers her fantasies mere whims or capricious thoughts, but more like the blessed whispers of what is possible and just moments away.

The bottom line; a woman who owns her own authentic sensuality is just damn sexy!

When I went in search of what some men thought authentic sensuality looked like, their answers were not only revealing, but came with great advice well worth heeding. I certainly have, and I suggest you do the same!

Antonio said: "My first thought is of this older woman I met on holiday in Ibiza Spain. Her laugh, her attitude, her chutzpah and obvious passion for life makes her irresistible! Surrounded by women augmented to look younger, it was her dynamic self-assurance that made her look ageless, sexy and so appealing. That's Authentic Sensuality!

Jack said: "For me, the paramount quality that makes a woman sensual is her outlook on life. If she laughs without measure, you know she derives great joy from life, has the ability to transcend pain and grief and find pleasure in the mere fact of her existence. Is this not the most appealing element of any human -- their ability to feel and express joy? To me, this is the most captivating virtue and one which, in my mind, is infinitely sensual."

Harry said: "Sensuality, opposed to sexuality, is something that comes from the inside out, and I almost think you are born with it. Because when it is authentic it becomes a part of everything you do; the way you speak, the way you move, the way you dance, the way you eat, the way you say nothing. Being authentic is the secret to being confident, and nothing is more sensual than an authentically confident woman."

These gentlemen spoke of qualities that go way beyond the perfection of the outer appearance that magazines and television shows seem to emphasize as "the most important part" of being beautiful to the opposite sex. The parts or pieces that seem to stop them in their tracks were qualities that were originally sourced from within. Each saw *Authentic Sensuality* more as an attitude than any obvious overt action or outward enhancement.

So if you also admire the Sofia's and J.Lo's of the world, and wouldn't mind it a bit if someone saw you as a ripe woman authentically sensual, I suggest that you begin to incorporate some of these hints into your persona and see what happens. The privilege of a lifetime is to become who you truly are, and being *Authentically Sensuality* is a great place to begin.

En-JOY!

"A happy person is not a person in a certain set of circumstances, but rather a person with a certain set of attitudes."

Hugh Downs

HOW TO HAVE GREAT SEX!
It's ALL in the ATTITUDE...

"Excellence is not a skill, It's an Attitude"
Ralph Marston

Since I know that my readers are the kind of people interested in having great sex, it seemed as the perfect place to discuss a very important piece for having an extraordinary life: *Your Attitude.* Yes, Dear Ones, I will be sharing some amazing tips on having great sex that I've gotten from experts with great resumes, but if you want anything ordinary to become your Everything Extraordinary, it all begins and ends, with a thought ~and your *Attitude* is created by your thoughts.

So let's start at the beginning. In psychology the word *Attitude* is an expression of favor or disfavor toward a person, a place or thing, a point of view. Basically your *Attitude* has three components that are demonstrated by what you think, what you do and what you feel.

No matter what is going on in your life you have various thoughts, opinions and beliefs about it, which produce an emotional response and a certain way of behaving accordingly. That's your *Attitude.* If your attitude in most situations makes you happy and is positively working for you, that's wonderful. But if

129

not, and you want to change your attitude, you have to change your thinking, the way you act or the way you feel. As Winston Churchill said, *"Attitude* is a little thing that makes a big difference."

So let's take this slow and easy and begin with some pillow talk about your attitude that can make all the difference, especially when it comes to your love life. Your thoughts affect your *Attitude* about everything you do. It affects how you see people, how people see you, and how you see yourself.

It affects how you view events and circumstances. It affects how you react to compliments and rejection, suggestions and criticisms. It affects all kinds of things that can come into play leading up to and then in the bedroom.

Your *Attitude* is more important than any fact or "figure," literally and figuratively speaking. It is more important than your history, your education, your possessions, your circumstances, successes, failures, or what other people think, say or do. With the right attitude you can turn a loss into a major win, a rejection into a blessed gift. It can even turn a frog into a prince.

Every moment of everyday you have choices in regard to the attitude you have about everything. You cannot change your past... you cannot change the fact that people will act in a certain way...you cannot change what is inevitable. But you can change what you do to make sure that all of your thoughts and perceptions are directed at positively influencing your attitude. In fact, *you* are the only person who can. Your *Attitude* governs the way you perceive everything and everyone, as well as the way everyone perceive you. All your moment to moment experiences depend on where your mind is at any given moment, and each of those experiences are determined by your perception.

So when it comes to lovemaking, it's not so much about what you are doing as it is about your *Attitude* about what you are doing that makes the difference about your experience; Before, During, and After.

BEFORE....

Before, which is often referred to as *Foreplay,* refers to activities that precede love-making or intercourse. One version of intercourse is called "social," which is any kind of human communication and/or interaction. The other form is sexual intercourse, which is where the *before* I am referring to comes in.

Great sex begins with different kinds of foreplay that happens way *before* a hand is touched or lips ever meet. It can start with eye contact that lasts a few seconds longer than normal; it can be a flirtatious remark or a touching compliment given during a follow-up phone call or morning text. It's the flowers, little gifts or obvious efforts put into a date or special day plans. Foreplay is all about building an emotional connection and getting some excitement going.

Having a great emotional connection starts with good communication, and good communication starts with TALKING; an essential piece in creating a relationship that includes good loving. Talking about your real and true self, not from "the resume" that you use to impress strangers is so important if you are interested in more than just a good roll in the hay. When you honestly can share parts of your life, it will encourage your partner to do the same, and that way you'll know more about each other that can lead to greater intimacy.

It's also important to LISTEN intently so you can hear what the heart is telling you. When you can listen empathetically you will be treating others as you would like to be treated, and that is what it's all about. "If you do this in a sensitive and sincere manner, believe it or not, you'll just have had some great foreplay. Before you can have great sex you need to start with great foreplay. And that starts with touching someone emotionally."

Foreplay is very important in helping to keep partners connected physically and emotionally, and definitely will go a long way toward great sex. Foreplay, in all its forms, is so that both of you are more comfortable and get more pleasure out of your love-making and each other, in and out of the bedroom. That is why your *Attitude* about it is so important.

As far as the actual physical actions involved with foreplay, you can't know what your partner likes and wants if you don't talk about it. People don't spend enough time talking to each other when they're not having sex.

So asking your partner questions about how they want to be touched, stroked, kissed, and caressed before you even get into bed, can go a long way to feeling at ease and comfortable with your partner. And for the record, it's also easier to have those conversations when you're not just about to have sex.

DURING...

In looking back over my own life experiences and from speaking to literally thousands of women and men around the world over the years, our greatest lovers... our most memorable experiences...the ones that will always have a front row seat in our hearts and minds, had nothing to do with specific talents or an arsenal of skills brought to "the party," but *everything* to do with how that person made us feel about ourselves when we were with them. And that is all *Attitude.*

Great sex happens when each partner makes the other feel as if they are truly desired, honored and appreciated for themselves, and that everything about them is just fine. When a woman or man feels as if their body and their expertise or even the lack of it is perfect, that they can freely express themselves all the time~ that's sexy!

Sex is a shared experience; the more you give of yourself the more you'll get in return. This is where your *Attitude* about the effort you put into foreplay comes in. Caring about the what, where and how someone likes to be touched, kissed, caressed, licked, what positions or acts they prefer or not, can make you "the best lover yet,' which of course, leads to "the best sex ever!"

133

Even though you might think that what you are doing is pretty great already, don't be afraid to experiment. This doesn't mean you have to recreate 50 shades of Grey, unless of course you want to (then go for it!), but a little experimentation can go a long way. Make variety the spice of your sex life and watch what happens! Try inventing your own private unique sexual language of love. Make up silly words that don't even make sense, except between the two of you. This is another way to personalize and individualize the lovemaking, and to demonstrate to your lover the exclusivity of your relationship.

Try different positions and other new variations on the age-old theme. You might even consider other areas than the bedroom to play in. Maybe move the action to the kitchen, living room or go outside on the deck, weather permitting. The point is that even the most exciting endeavor can become boring." Try something new; then in six months, when hanging from the chandelier becomes boring, position three is exciting!

Just show respect for what comes naturally. If you initiate some action and get a vibe that this is not in your partner's comfort zone, the respectful thing to do is back off and let it go. Let them be the expert in their pleasure. Guess what? They know what they like better than you do. If you are not sure what they actually want, then ask. "Do you like this, would you prefer me doing that?" Be attentive to what is bringing your partner pleasure. Just remember, a sign of respect to how your partner is actually feeling, can really score points.

By allowing your partner the space to step back and look at doing something different gives them the freedom to acquiesce at possibly a later date, which can lead to something even better!

Planning unplanned time when nothing has to happen can be a real turn-on, especially since this is where real contact is made. It lets a person know that you want to be with them for who they are, not for another dinner or simply as your sex toy. Yes ladies, guys feel that way as well, if sex always is your main interest or attraction!

Now that you have some great tips on what to do, as promised, I want to get back to your *Attitude,* just to make sure you've got your A-Game on.

Unfortunately a lot of women have had some very disappointing love affairs that have left them scarred and damaged. Unconsciously, in the sense that they don't even realize their underlying *attitude* adopted for "most" of the available population. Throw-off remarks infer that they are seeing all potential partners in a negative light. As if they are waiting for the other shoe to drop and the next encounter to go terribly wrong.

Eventually this resentful *Attitude* will chase away some really good people who might have been a great match. And if they do attract someone and go into the relationship with this negative *attitude i*t can potentially spill over into the bedroom. "Faking it till you Make it" is a great idea when you're turning around a mindset, but it's a really lousy concept to bring into the bedroom.

So if you are in bed "wishing this 'thing' was over already" and finding problems instead of promises for enjoyment, trust me when I say, the other person *will* feel it. If you are in a situation that is designed to make you happy and you're not, then you need to look at the source of your *Attitude*. Because clearly, you have some sort of resistance to your being pleasured from past conditioning or experiences, *or* you're in the wrong bed!

But fortunately, that particular *Attitude* i*s* not a terminal disease. If it's your issue and you truly have a desire to change it, it can be changed. The first step is to be aware that this *Attitude* is holding you back from fully having and enjoying the kind of life and loving you deserve. Breaking a mindset can be difficult, but the longer you hold on to it, the more deeply ingrained it can become.

AFTER...

So let's start with your physicality, as your body is a huge influence on your mind-set. How you feel about your body affects how you move in the world and certainly what you bring to bed. If you're not feeling so hot about yourself or are still attached to a former lover's critical evaluation of your natural assets, now is the perfect time to change your positive *Attitude*.

Here is where I am a huge proponent of "Fake it until you Make it." Assuming the new *Attitude* that "you're awesome and you know it," while you are still working on "perfecting yourself", with practice, you will begin to change your negative beliefs into affirming ones.

Always remember this one Very Important Thing: Only you know how you really feel about anything. Only you know if you "are Faking it till you Make it" and only you will know when you go from "I am just OK," to "I am really fabulous!" And please don't think that you are being arrogant by loving yourself, because trust me, you are not. The Universe requires *that You Love You* unconditionally. If you don't love all of you, why should anyone else?

When you can learn to love yourself completely "*as is*," forgiving yourself and let go of any perceived flaws or faults, you will be naturally confident. Nothing is more attractive, no seemly perfection of any feature or body part, than a totally confident individual who has no doubt who they are or what they bring to the party. You become a gift to all men and women.

Which brings me to a subject *of Abundance,* one of the most important *Attitudes* to develop and is sadly lacking in lots of men and women, especially around attracting a special partner. Because of this negative propaganda, many individuals tend to come from a scarcity mentality around quality partners, especially when it comes to dating. Such a mentality is poisonous. The idea that there are" only so many good ones left," leaves you feeling as if anyone who might rejected you, in one way or another, is just another example of the ever-shrinking pool of available quality companions.

This *Attitude* makes you put too much effort, attention and even "forever more" intentions on one particular person who may not even be right for you. This terribly misguided *Attitude* that "there's not much out there so I'd better grab what I can or I'll be all alone because no one good will be left," is like stacking the deck against you, way before the game even begins!

Of course this is ridiculous, and a woman or man with a healthy abundance mentality, fully understands this at an instinctive level and believes this to the core of their being. The truth of it is, when you start to live from the *Attitude* of "this one or better," you stop putting such importance on just one person. So when things go badly in a romance, or they turn out not to be who you thought they were, it may hurt, but that's part of the process. There are literally millions of others "friends" out there, possibly just around the corner, eager to meet you. As my friend Marie's mom always says, "Once you get the wrong man out of the door the right man can get into the room!"

Imagine how you would feel if your truth was that you have an almost endless number of opportunities to find the love you want. How would you feel if you believed that you had more options than you had ever imagined? Well start to believe it, because it's that exact *Attitude* that will let you joyfully attract the perfect mate for you.

Your perspective, point of view, belief, mind-set or philosophy about life is what will ultimately design and define all of your experiences. I know I have said this before, but it's so worth repeating: the circumstances of your life actually matter less to your happiness than the sense of control you feel over those circumstances!

The *Attitude* you have *about everything* is what defines your life. Once you become consciously aware of what beliefs are directing your actions and reactions, and then master the ability to reframe the ones that don't serve you into ones that do, you will possess the secret to unending joy and happiness, and if you so desire, the Greatest Sex of your life!

En-JOY!

LIFE ~ **LUST** ~ and LOVE...

LOVE

"Love is Friendship that has caught fire. It is quiet understanding, confidence, mutual sharing and forgiving. It is loyalty through good and bad times. It makes allowances for human weaknesses and settles for less than perfection. It's like the wind, you can't see it but you can feel it."

The word "LOVE" has a variety of meanings... each depending on the subject matter and situation. Even though the essence of *Love* is frequently debated, with no conclusion, what I know for sure is that you can't have joy without *Love* and when you *Love* you are filled with Joy...sweet.

"Love is a decision, it is a judgment, it is a promise" to an object, animate or inanimate, a philosophy or life itself. More often than not, the depth of this emotion determines your state of happiness or joy.

As Anatole France said so perfectly, "you learn to speak by speaking, to study by studying, to run by running, to work by working; in just the same way, you learn to love by loving." It takes time to get it right, but if anything is worth your effort, it's *LOVE*.

"Lust is temporary, romance can be nice, but love is the most important thing of all. Because without love... lust and romance will always be short-lived."

Danielle Steele

LOVE...

"How do you spell Love?
You don't spell it...You feel it."
Winnie the Pooh~A.A. Milne

Love, Love, Love, Love, Love... I could repeat that word over and over again... and each time my mind comes up with a different form of it that activates yet another delicious sense.

At the moment I am writing the last pieces of this book that will be handed over to my editor and then my publisher within just a few days. Sitting on my bed with my computer balanced on a table that is on top of a pillow stretched over my legs, I am bolstered up with lots and lots of pillows. There is a yummy lavender scented candle and a vase of flowers nearby, and my favorite singers playing their music in the background is keeping me company... and I am in LOVE... with this precise piece of my life.

This scene I just described is definitely *not* what anyone who knows me would visualize as my writing desk or what would bring me such happiness. And that makes me really chuckle. Because it is just one of a million examples of how I or anyone can experience this feeling called LOVE. In these last few precious days of birthing my book, I see that I am in the stages of falling in love...and it's blissful.

I am *lusting* after each hour left in order for me to meet my deadline, insatiably wanting more, and not wanting the night to end. The undeniable *infatuation* I have for all the support I've received, both physically and spiritually in helping me create this new book with the opportunity to share my "secrets" and touch the hearts and expand the minds of men and women all over the world, is utterly intoxicating. I am absolutely *joyfully in LOVE!*

So what is LOVE?

Most people think of LOVE as a verb, "a feeling that is displayed in many actions, and serves to indicate the occurrence or performance of an action. Certain kinds of expressed feelings, that most people experience when in Love." That is a fine explanation, except it's not quite the whole truth.

Yes, it's true, LOVE is a "doing" word that can convey a physical or mental action, or a state of being, but that is just too simplistic an answer. Love originates as a noun that necessarily produces verbs. *Love at its source* creates it all, including everyone and everything. Our actions are merely manifestations of that Love.

To manifest Love you need to understand that LOVE is first and foremost created in your mind. Your most important on-going work is to learn to Love yourself so completely you are never in need of someone else to complete you. Whoever you are and whatever you have done or are doing, trust me when I say, right now, *YOU* are enough just as you are.

Once I realized that the quality and quantity of LOVE I received from others was a direct reflection of how much, or how little, I truly loved and cared for myself, I made loving *all of myself* a top priority. The moment I began to assume the responsibilities of that job, was the moment I began to attract the quality of people who were capable and wanted to love me as I had learned to love myself.

When it comes to the heart, in order to receive LOVE from another, it must first be expressed as an action. Behaving lovingly towards another, shows that we love that person, and when they behave lovingly in return, we feel loved. But just like you can *talk* loving without really loving, you can *act* loving without really loving.

So no matter what you are doing with whomever you are doing it with, if you are fully living in the joy of the present moment with an awareness of all the abundance within that moment, it becomes easy to obliterate any negative thoughts and feelings. Being in the moment with a sense of LOVE opens your heart to gratitude, kindness and loving energy.

What I've realized from my numerous workshops and coaching sessions is that when someone comes to me with the question, "what is LOVE?" it usually means something is lacking. They are either feeling uneasy about their responses within a relationship, lust and infatuation, or they are trying to figure out whether their romantic interest really loves them *or* if they are really in love with their romantic interest. On occasion, it can come from the desire to find LOVE, with the belief that a better understanding of it will help them identify it, just in case it's standing right in front of them.

Food for thought: Why do you think that it takes a sense of lack before most people will begin to analyze and contemplate such a huge life-changing important emotion as LOVE? It's such a shame since we want more positive, not negative thoughts to attract the same.

LOVE is a choice. There is tangible proof. It's not an abstract thought or obtuse feeling. It is concrete and evidence that it is built on a strong foundation formed by your intent to be the best version of you.

In Romantic LOVE, you know that you have chosen Love once you have decided to enhance the experience by taking the time to learn about another person. When you can appreciate and accept all their best qualities, idiosyncrasies and differences...when you can allow each other to be yourself without trying to change the other... you will know that you have chosen Love.

It's easy to choose love when things are going really well, but it's a worthier gift when fears and insecurities come up. Choosing LOVE over fear is when our greatest growth happens. Feelings can be deceptive. Sometimes, what you perceive as Love may in fact be just another emotion. But actions cannot be mistaken.

So, rather than ask, "What is LOVE?" you might ask yourself, "Have I Loved enough? Do I perform acts of Love whenever possible? Do I allow myself to receive Love in return?" If you want Love, you must show it.

Which brings us to savvy Veronica's research on Falling in Love~ Stage 3: Deep *Love and Attachment.*

"There is documented scientific research on the kind of changes that come over you when you engage in any way on any level with any kind of *loving.* For example, when two people have gotten to know each other and gone beyond the lust and infatuation phase and now are seeing each other's "complete" personality, including all their bits and pieces and still have made the choice to love and accept each other, a neuro-hormone in the form of Love floods the body. Oxytocin is often called the 'commitment hormone,' because it's released during orgasm and is believed to enhance the desire for more coupling when you are intimate.

"Where there is love there is madness," Socrates said, and once you know that romantic LOVE and addiction share similar brain chemistry, you can see why! So if you really are not interested in a serious committed relationship, you may consider thinking twice before you casually sleep with your next attraction.

Because your brain is wired to bond and connect with a partner when you've experienced pleasure, the varied emotions of lust and infatuation have so much more power over your romantic choices. Remember this the next time you are tempted to play with that hot bad boy or sexy girl.

LOVE will urge you to find a balance, while lust will want all of your attention and act up when its needs are not being met. Lust is great in its place, but it's not Love.

Lust is selfish. It thinks only of itself. The only reason you think about that person so much is because of what they can do for you. Lust is obsessed with the physical, while real LOVE takes time to develop.

It's that confusion between the two that leads to all sorts of problems further down the road, especially once you've both returned to the set-point of your comfort zone. Fortuitously, most of us can move through lust to to love and, if you're really lucky, the lust stays on as the love deepens.

Enjoy the journey of self-discovery from someone for whom you lust to someone you could love. Don't rush it; allow it to unfold naturally. LOVE takes her time; she's not into quickie. There is no way to make a person love you. That's why actions really do speak louder than words. If the chemistry is right, the lust will transform into romantic love.

When you are really loved, you feel it intuitively in your gut, because your heart takes cues from your senses. Our sensory organs report to our brain and our brain will interpret the data and sends on the report to our heart. You don't need to deeply contemplate or ask questions, just notice. Do you receive loving smiles, kind complimentary words or tender touches? The brain will process this information and rightfully conclude, "You are being LOVED."

But let's get something clear- no matter what the movies and novels want us to believe; LOVE at first sight doesn't really exist. Sexual attraction is such a huge part of dating that it's not surprising many of us get confused between what is Love and what is Lust.

Real Love, True Love, Deep Love doesn't want to own, control or possess you. It wants you to always feel supported, honored, cherished and encouraged. It is the desire to see yourself and the person you care for grow into the best people you can possibly be, no matter what, under all circumstances. So the more honesty and passion you can bring into your own self-relationship, the easier it will be to attract someone who shares those same qualities.

LOVE, Love, Love, Love... in all its various forms *is* the greatest of the God-given gifts. It is everywhere. "It is the essence we breathe, the essence of our heartbeat." It has all the power to add to, change, even alter and transform difficult challenges and circumstances into golden opportunities that make your wildest dreams come true. It can turn strangers into life partners and the best of friends. And JOY... is the beautiful voice of LOVE heard around the world that is remembered forever.

En-JOY!

"Love is a force more formidable than any other. It is invisible - it cannot be seen or measured, yet it is powerful enough to transform you in a moment, and offer you more joy than any material possession possibly could."

Barbara de Angelis

WHAT'S LOVE GOT TO DO WITH IT?

"Love is an irresistible desire to be irresistibly desired."
Mark Twain

If there is one topic that men and women are really confused about, it's LOVE. Where do you go to find it and how do you deal with it once you do? Then, once you have it, how can you tell if it's the real thing; i.e. True Love? Whew, it's exhausting! Yet because we all so want to love and be loved in return, too often we end up with what my grooviest role-model calls a second-hand emotion.

Tina Turner, Rock Star Extraordinaire, is one steaming hot seasoned woman. With her natural charisma and high-energy performances offering the kind of music that makes you want to jump up and dance, I instantly became a devotee. But what made her my real heroine was watching her courageous passage from being fearful, dependent, and terribly abused, to becoming a self-reliant, confident, still loving, ageless beauty. Observing her process for regaining power in order to have her best life ever, continues to inspire me when confronted with any challenging or difficult times.

So it seemed beyond perfect when my dear friend felt
the need to once again retell the destructive demise of
her very long live-in relationship, ended her venting
with, "and it hurts so much because I still love him." It
was at that exact moment when Tina's words of wisdom
came spilling out from the speakers giving her the
perfect answer.

*"You must understand, though the touch of your
hand makes my pulse react... That it's only the thrill
of boy meeting girl...*

*Opposites attract ~ It's physical ~ Only logical You
must try to ignore that it means more than that...*

What's love got to do, got to do with it?
What's love, but a second-hand emotion?
What's love got to do, got to do with it?
Who needs a heart when a heart can be broken?"

And there I was, off and running, channeling what
I just knew my girl Tina would say.

"What's love got to do with it?" I asked my friend,
"Sweetheart, if you think this is love, you have no idea
what love is. Real love doesn't hurt or cause you pain.
True love gives you a sense of peace and security that
makes you feel safe, even in the storm. If it hurts, it's
something else. But it sure isn't love."

"It could be the fear of being alone," I continued, "the need to be in a relationship, part of a couple. Maybe it's by associating with someone who has attributes that you believe you lack, such as financial wealth, social status or a really fun-loving magnetic personality that makes you feel more important. It could be an addiction to bad behavior, treatment so familiar it's become your comfort zone. Thanks to a family member, former partner or lover, you think that this is normal and the best you deserve. But whatever it is, no one's heart ever aches from love, only from a lack of it."

As the song went into the next verse, my message was reinforced.

"I've been taking on a new direction, but I have to say... I've been thinking about my own protection and it scares me to feel this way."

"Ah, then there's Passion, Lust and Desire," I went on, "which in the best of times can cause havoc. In the worst of situations it is a form of jealousy and possessiveness, which definitely is not evidence of love. Love doesn't drive people crazy it brings you to a sense of calm and sanity. It's not controlling or grasping, but generous and freeing."

"Can you have passion and desire for someone you truly love?" my dear friend asked.

"Absolutely!" I sang out.

"Chemistry is very important, but recognizing the difference between a craving and real love is vital.

Allowing your over-active pheromones to be the choice maker of your next great love can be a very dangerous thing. Especially since it has been scientifically proven that the average life span of a romantic obsession is two years!"

"But how do you distinguish between what is true love and what isn't?" she cried out in despair.

"True Love can't begin until the *in-love* experience has run its course. When you are in-love, you believe that your beloved can do no wrong and has discovered the key to your heart's desire. In reality, each of you is only responding to the other's signals on how to be satisfied. But at some point, things settle down and then the real person shows up. That's why Dr. Joyce Brothers was right when she said, "*No matter how lovesick a woman is, she shouldn't take the first pill that comes along!*"

At the heart of it all, we are all romantic fools with "an irresistible desire to be irresistibly desired," each one desperately wanting our love story to be *the one* that defies all logic. So how do you find that most precious thing: someone to love and be truly loved in return?

Well, as Albert Einstein said, "It is the supreme art of the teacher to awaken joy in creative expression and knowledge." That is exactly what I now intend to do.

A SAVVY WOMAN'S SECRETS FOR ATTRACTING TRUE LOVE

1. *Start by loving yourself unabashedly* and without restrain. Become your most attentive lover, and you can attract a true love from want and not need.

2. *Open your heart to what's possible.* Begin to take down the walls that have "protected you" from receiving the kind of love you desire and deserve.

3. *Stop, Look, and Listen* for the signs of real love that won't take no for an answer and moves forward with positive actions.

4. *Seek out the best kind of relationship*; one where you are not only lovers, but trust-worthy best friends as well; someone who cares and supports your goals.

5. *Make Extraordinary your mirrored reflection.* Never give your love to anyone who treats you as if you are ordinary. Never settle for less than you give.

6. *Be and expect open-hearted acceptance.* When you Feel validated and approved of, it lights up the way for you to walk in the same direction toward happiness.

7. *Have enough courage to trust loving one more time, and possibly even one more time again.*

Tina might be right, "LOVE is nothing but a silly old fashioned notion," but it's also the closest thing we have to magic. So *"What's love got to do with it?"* Simply Everything!   *En-JOY!*

"I've heard that people stand in bad situations because a relationship like that gets turned up by degrees. It is said that a frog will jump out of a pot of boiling water. Place him in a pot and turn it up a little at a time, and he will stay until he is boiled to death. Us frogs understand this."

Deb Caletti

SUNDAY to SUNDAY ROMANCE
~ ABUSE RED FLAGS ~

"Suffering usually relates to wanting things to be different from the way they are."

Allow me to introduce you to *My Girls*. A couple of truly extraordinary savvy women who, among other things, taught me one of the most important lessons: How to avoid getting involved with the worst kind of person: a Toxic Abuser.

First there is the spectacular and sensational Suzana; an entrepreneur, gifted artist and connoisseur of life. A woman who has danced the light fandango wearing many different chapeaus: ingénue, fashion muse, savvy businesswoman, beloved sister, mother, grandmother, philanthropist and most recently, sizzling femme fatale. A self-assured and confident woman who slithers in and out of fascinating and exciting life experiences, like a sleek black jaguar finessing any falls or slips along the way, with few, if any visible injuries; a talent I have been trying to emulate for years!

And then there is my adored Annabel. Annabel is like a shooting-star. Filled with a vivacious sparkling energy that draws everyone to her generous and enchanting personality, regardless of their status, age, race or color; she's simply delicious. A well-respected psychologist and writer, her free-spirited, rule-breaking and rule-making personality inspires you to be better.

Where Suzana always jumps in with both feet and then figures out how to swim, Annabel is much more cautious. Even though she warmly welcomes others into her life, she carefully observes their words and actions before she decides if they are going to be a real friend, a lover, just another acquaintance, or someone she just used to know.

As dear friends and committed teachers and mentors to my personal growth, their friendship is priceless. We meet for dinner every few months or so and the drill is pretty much the same. After settling in with another scrumptious meal and a great bottle of wine, Suzana slowly begins to delight us with the latest chapter of her long running novella. Wrapped in ribbons of laughter and loving jabs, Annabel always interjects great insight, wisdom and life lessons that to this day have served me well. One of my favorite was dubbed "*The Sunday to Sunday Romance.*"

This episode was very different from others we have laughed over as it actually left Suzana a bit shaken. For the first time in her life she saw what an emotionally abusive relationship really looked like and just how vulnerable a woman or man can be to someone who is a narcissistically skilled manipulator. It so upset her, she actually met with experts to learn more about it and brought "her sisters" a story filled with Red Flags not to be missed!

She began...

"If this story was being told in the early 60's you would absolutely believe it had been the inspiration for the Shirlee's hit song *I met him on a Sunday*, as the lyrics say it all... minus the juicy details!"

"Well, I met him on a Sunday (oooh)...
And I spoke to him on Monday (oooh)...
Well, I dated him on a Tuesday (oooh)...
And I kissed him on Wednesday (oooh)...
He didn't come on Thursday (oooh)...
But I saw him on Friday (oooh)...
When he didn't showed up on Sunday (oooh)...
I said "Bye, Bye Baby (oooh)...
Doo ronde ronde ronde pa pa...
Doo ronde ronde ronde pa pa...
Doo ronde ronde ronde pa pa..."

What a hoot!

"Just like in the song, on Sunday I did say *Bye, Bye Baby (oooh)*, when all my senses literally screamed, '*Get me out of here!*' This was one of the craziest dating experiences I've ever had! Leaving me with no doubt that this is exactly what being emotionally abused looks like, which compelled me to very quickly learn as much as I could about it.

Suzana then went on to say, "But let me slow down a bit and start at the beginning, because it is within the flow of all the interactions from Sunday to Sunday that brings the message home. Fortunately, it was short but sweet!"

Suzana shifted in her chair, took a sip of wine and began her titillating tale again.

"I did meet him on a Sunday *(oooh),* as I was coming out of a noisy crowded fund-raiser for local musicians. John was quite a handsome fella who I noticed was noticing me when I was dancing with my friends. So I wasn't surprised to see him following me outside nor when he asked me if I had 'any other unmarried friends who were as pretty as I was.' This was an opportunity I couldn't refuse, and I started to ask him questions as if it was for one of my friends.

You see, ever since I've been single I've worn my wedding band when I go out. It tends to deter lots of jerks from hitting on me, and for the ones that do, it is used as the reason for a polite dismissal. When the occasion arises that I am interested and I tell the fella the reason for the ring, and they are always so flattered that I have deemed them worthy of my hard to garner attention. Being a 'grand prize' worth winning is a challenge we know all men just simply can't resist!"

This story was getting better with each new insight and I couldn't wait to hear what she had to say next.

"As Annabel repeatedly says, 'our gut instincts tells us what's really going on even when we chose to ignore it, especially when it contradicts a thought we have about something we think we want.'

But in my defense, it was the week before the most romantic holiday of the year, Valentine's Day, and I just didn't want to be home alone. I figured out early on that this guy and I were different in the way we live our lives; he does all sorts of outdoorsy activities every day, early to bed, early to rise, where I am a night owl who often prefers indulging in more of the indoor cultural arts.

He dislikes noisy crowded venues and prefers listening to music more than dancing. I, on the other hand, will dance to anything anywhere, and could care less about the venue. He also had some really weird specific eating habits besides the norm of no alcohol, no red meat, no sweets, etc. I personally love all forms of ethnic and creative cuisines, and almost nothing is off limits.

But he was awfully cute, new to town, and did present an opportunity for a unique adventure, which is my favorite thing. Besides, I saw it as a chance to try on a different lifestyle that could be to my liking. When he found out I was single, he immediately asked me out for the upcoming Valentine's Day. In that moment, I slipped inside my body and gently put an imaginary hand over the mouth of my natural instincts and told my gut feelings to take a hike...at least till after Friday!"

'Well, I dated him on Tuesday (*oooh)*' and had a great time. We went to a romantic Italian restaurant that was recommended by my healthy friends. When they didn't have one of the two foods he will eat at an Italian eatery, he proceeded to order a Sirloin steak, followed by a slice of rich chocolate cake! And here it begins; As just days before he had told me that he doesn't eat any red meat or sweets. At the time I didn't connect the dots, but technically speaking this is called, *Gas-lightening.*"

Hint #1: Abusers often practice Gas-Lighting.
This term refers to a form of mental abuse in which
opposing false information is presented with the intent
of making the victim doubt his or her own memory,
perception and sanity. The phrase was adopted from a
1930's movie where a husband kept turning the gas
lights on and off while repeatedly telling his wife she
did or didn't do it, intending to drive her crazy.

"Because I am the kind of gal that chooses to believe
I am so enticing that any man would so willingly want
to change his ways to keep me in his life." Susana said.
"I chose to see this new fella's change of heart around
his eating habits as proof of my magical powers!"

As always I was beyond enthralled, and sitting on the
edge of my chair to hear what happened next.

"Regardless of this confusing behavior, it was a lovely
evening, which included a bit of dancing afterwards with
a kiss good night. Throughout the day on Wednesday
and into the afternoon on Thursday I got lots of nice
emails and texts...until he asked me out for that night.
I had theater tickets, so I couldn't see him on Thursday
(*oooh*), but told him that I could meet him afterwards
at around 9:30 pm.

"When his responding email said 'this old man needs
his rest to be refreshed for Friday's date,' I responded
with a playful email, apologizing for sending this note to
the wrong fella, because the hot cute guy I was with the
other night certainly was not an old man. So if you see
him, tell that a short refreshing nap might help."

You can only imagine my shock to receive an email shortly afterwards that began with 'Sweetheart, this isn't going to work, because we are so very different'. Then it went on to list all the many things that are so different and implying that his staying out late and eating red meat and sweets was my fault! He ended his note with 'let's just be friends.' "

Hint #2: **Abusers tend to blame others for their shortcomings.** So if someone in your life seems to always be blaming everything on someone else, namely you, this is not a good sign and will probably only get worse.

"Because I was so dumbfounded with this 360 degree turn-around and the accusations about my character were so wrong, I couldn't resist sending back an email attempting to defend my behavior, explaining who my true character. Even though I knew I had nothing to defend, at that point I wanted us to just be friends.

Hint #3: **Abusers instill defensiveness fear and by attempting to intimidate you** with dominance, violence or power tactics in order to control you and keep you under their spell.

The following morning I woke up to discover another email from him.

"Thank you Suzana for your very insightfulness and forthright explanation. Now that I see that we do have so many similarities, if you are still willing, I would love to pick you up for dinner tonight. But don't expect any flowers, as I prefer something more personal.' Since I chose to believe that my well-written note had cleared up a simply misunderstanding, I happily agreed."

"Well I dated him on Friday (*oooh*), and had an over-the-top Valentine's Day, definitely one of my top three! He looked very handsome in his well-tailored suit with a blue shirt that matched his eyes. When he got out of his snazzy car the first thing he handed me was a large bouquet of flowers in a beautiful vase, after specifically telling me he *was not* going to bring me flowers. He then reached in the back seat for a large bag that he proceeded to bring into the house. *Hmmm...*

Because of our 'rough beginning,' he had requested that we have some time to reacquaint ourselves before going off to a crowded restaurant. I bought a bottle of sparkling Elderberry juice for my new non-drinking friend. So imagine my surprise when the first thing he brought out of his bag was a bottle of a really good cabernet, which he insisted I open, and then proceeded to drink almost half of it!"

Hint #4: **Abusers tend to abuse substances and lie about using them**. Not all abusers abuse drugs or drink excessive amounts of alcohol, but many do and may try to hide it. Their addictions often lead to erratic behavior.

"As we settled in with our glasses of wine, he reached into his bag to bring out one fabulous gift after another. First it was a large red satin heart shaped box filled with expensive chocolates. Next came a beautifully wrapped box of customized artistic truffles, followed by a lovely basket filled with all sorts of scented bath and body products, and last, but not least, silk lingerie from VS!

Holy moly, if this was how he treated me on our second date, after just a small misunderstanding, what would my birthday be like? LOL, as they say."

This story was getting better and better, and already I was learning so much!

"By the time we left for our dinner reservations at an upscale restaurant, things had gotten so much better and continued into the night with hours of fun flirty conversations, lots of laughter and good times. We then moved on to his choice of a 'noisy venue,' where he insisted we stay and 'dance.'

For the record, I was ready to go home for a bit of romance, but he seemed hell-bent on showing me just how important I was to him by completely altering and changing all of his rules and regulations! Well, if that was true, I wasn't going to stop him, and chose to revel in my obviously charismatic charms.

Hint #5: **Abusers use gifts and many heartfelt apologies** to smooth over past actions and lower your resistance to being abused again.

"We eventually did go to my home for a little bit of romancing, and I had to just about throw out my early-to- bed guy at 1:30 AM, after he asked me to spend the next day with him to go to some local fairs. I said yes, but I would have to be home on the early side, as I had dinner plans with a friend and her sick husband.

165

Even though we had a very nice time, the cracks were beginning to show. While we were walking around he started to make little remarks about my behavior. Such as my unnecessary overly warm response to friends we saw, or that I was the only one who applauded the very good street musician and wanted to know if that kind of behavior was really all necessary?

He didn't just hold my hand like a boyfriend, but tightly like a father who doesn't want his child to leave his sight. It felt very uncomfortable and definitely controlling. When I tried to get him to release my hand and he only held it tighter! He clearly had an agenda that I was not following."

Hint #6: **Abusers are controlling and will often get physical** after emotionally abusing. If you are in an emotionally abusive relationship, there is a good chance that eventually things may get physical. At first the toxic abuser might grab, push or pin you down in a bruising way. This can quickly and unexpectedly accelerate.

When Susana stopped to take another sip of her wine, my body responded with a small jolt of a sense of being brought back to the moment. I was so mesmerized with the story and the descriptions of various actions I never thought to link to these forms of abuse and I could barely wait for her to begin again.

"As you know, I like everybody and my friends love that about me. I am often complimented on warmly welcoming friends or soon to be friends with a hug or kiss. It is one of my favorite and often most admired characteristic. The idea that a man in my life might actually disapprove of my behavior or not want anyone else to benefit from my attention never dawned on me. And to not properly acknowledge an artist for their talent and efforts, being one myself would be physically impossible ...almost rude or insensitive."

Hint #7: **Abusers are often possessive and extremely jealous**. Prominent traits of abusers are that their jealousy over their partner paying attention to anyone else, or someone giving their attention to you. They also tend to be extremely jealous of your personal good qualities, dreams and goals. Their jealousy and rage over intangible things stem from their narcissism and lack of control they feel over all aspects of your life.

"Before we even began the day, I had told him that I needed to be back by a certain time because I had been invited to a friend's for dinner. Yet in the middle of this seemly lovely day, he asked me if I could stay longer at the fair as well as see him again later that night, subtly reminding me of his desire to have a relationship with a partner that had lots of time for him, as opposed to the last one who had many priorities other than him."

"So to appease him I sent a text to my friend asking if there would be a problem if I came later and left earlier. The response was 'Yes. It would be a problem. I have planned something special.' So my response to her was, 'I will be there on time and leave when you kick me out!' And to him I said, 'Sorry Sweetie, I can't, my plans with my friends are set in stone.' "

"He 'seemed' to understand and even texted me later telling me how much he enjoyed our day together and was sorry he couldn't be with me tonight. He then asked me to brunch the next day, which I hesitantly agreed.

Hint #8: **Abusers only want to have you for themselves**. They do not want to understand that you have a life outside of the relationship that includes any family and friends. They must and only want to be your main priority.

"Because we had sweet goodbyes and nice texts, I did agree to see him again tomorrow afternoon. I didn't get it then, but I sure did when I got the next and final (as far as I was concerned) email."

Hint #9: **Abusers punish you for time away**. This goes along with the isolation technique: Abusers want you all to themselves. If you have any other plans or go somewhere or do something without them, they will find a way to punish you later.

"Imagine my utter surprise and shock when I turned on my phone the next day only to see an email waiting that had been sent at 4:45 am.

It began: 'Sweetheart, you know how much I like you and the willingness I've shown to accommodate, change and come around to your way. If you care about me, you will do the same for me.'

Then the next two or three paragraphs had a litany of make-wrongs about every aspect of my personality and core being! Which included that I had better start taking my physical exercise more seriously as one day I would surely spread. And that could be very unappealing.' Imagine saying that to anyone, especially me!"

Hint #10: **Abusers are nasty name callers**, joking or not, they mean to hurt you and keep you in line. Toxic abusers often cover themselves by blaming you, saying that you need to lighten up or that you are too sensitive.

When he showed up on Sunday, I said 'Bye, Bye Baby *(oooh)...Baby good-by!'*

Doo ronde ronde ronde pa pa......
Doo ronde ronde ronde pa pa......
Doo ronde ronde ronde pa pa......

"A person can do lots of things that I could possibly overlook, and I really welcome being shown another way that would make me a better person. But not getting the core of my essence, and wanting me to change the characteristics I am most proud of and have literally been honing over a lifetime, is a definite deal breaker! To that I have only one thing to say; *Bye, Bye Baby... oooh!... Baby Good-bye for Good... oooh, oooh... OOOH!"*

The first words out of wise and astute Anabel's mouth directed at me, after I collapsed in my chair in total hysterics were; "Sweetheart, I know Susana tells a great story, but don't miss the important message; when your gut is telling you something is off you need to listen to and pay attention. You need to stop and ask yourself, what's really going on here? What am I missing?

Sometimes these feelings are nothing more than a knee-jerk reaction to a memory of something or someone from your past and have nothing to do with this new guy or gal. But you can only properly assess that once you have taken some time to step back and analyze what's going on.

Sure, anyone would have been thrown off their game by all the different highs and lows Susana experienced in her Sunday-to-Sunday romance. It definitely was bizarre. But if the real truth be told, somewhere within the first few hours of being with this man, I would bet there were tell-tale signs."

Susanna nodded in agreement. Anabel was right-on about having feelings that something was off. She admittedly chose to ignore the signs because of the "Valentine's Day Golden Carrot" waved in her face!

"We all want to be loved and have the fairytale life that we see in the movies and read about in novels. So when a master manipulator waves shiny golden carrots in front of your face: good looking, wealthy, generous, attentive, fun-loving or any other quality that's on your personal wish list, the best of us can get blinded by the bling and ignore the flashing signals our gut is sending.

Because these master manipulators usually imply 'that we are the one woman that they have been searching for their entire lives, the one person who can finally make them a happier and better person. Our ego gets excited trying to prove them right. Never realizing that it is impossible. They don't really want to be changed."

Anabel when on to say "their narcissism and need to abuse another to feel bigger and better is their pleasure, and you have just become their latest conquest. The many variations of sweet words and forms of 'loving" are how they slowly begin the process of weaving their beautiful silky-soft threaded webs. Once they have caught you and are holding you tightly in their grasp, it can be very difficult to find the good sense, wisdom and courage to get free and reclaim your life."

The message of this story is about encouraging women to respect your intuitions and pay attention to your wise inner voice. To never ignore the red flags that your gut is waving in your face, where intuitively you know danger exists. It's about always affirming your self-respect and self-worth so that you're not easily seduced by faux "Gold Covered" dreams or over-the-top promises that all form of master manipulators and abusers use to draw you into their seductive and deceitful webs.

It's also about not forgetting that the world really is filled with lots of good caring people who would never intentionally hurt another person~ men and women who also want to genuinely love and be loved in return. By keeping your eyes, ears and heart open to the good guys, Sunday can become your favorite day of the week!

En-JOY!

"I want to tell women that you need to love yourself and make yourself a priority. It's only when you are happy yourself, can you make everyone else around you happy. I am still a dreamer and still believe in fairy tales, but there is only that much one should give another person. You need to keep something for yourself."

Bipasha Bas

HOW TO FALL MADLY IN LOVE
with You!

"I have an everyday religion that works for me. Love yourself first and everything else falls into line." Lucille Ball

"Youth is wasted on the young," so they say. But I've always known that nothing is ever wasted and it's been my lifetime mission to prove it wrong.

As a little girl, I had lots of indefinable aspirations. When any grown-up would bend down and sweetly ask me, "What do you want to be when you grow up?" I'd answer with a big smile on my face, "I don't know, but for sure I am going to be doing something special!" I didn't know what, but I innately knew that my education to "do something special" wasn't going to come from kids my own age or from formal schooling, but from more seasoned enthusiasts of the University of Life.

I always thought my parents had just the coolest, brightest, most interesting friends who always seemed enthusiastic about everything. Whenever I was lucky enough to get access to this esteemed group, I would try to melt into the background so no one would notice me and suggest I be sent off to bed. I was obsessed with wanting to look and listen for precious pearls of insights that would be dropped into my formative mind.

Like the mouse that stole the cheese, I would sneak away to savor each and every morsel, trying my best many times and over the years to incorporate their paramount attributes into my way of being. These gems definitely embellished my proverbial crown, but the shiny platinum setting came thanks to my incredible parents, especially my mom, Ketsy.

Ketsy, which loosely means "cute little kitten" in Yiddish, wasn't a Betty Crocker or Leave It to Beaver kind of mom. She was an exquisite beauty with a quick mind and the know-how to create a beautiful home that welcomed all, no matter their age, race or status. It was a place everyone loved coming to and I loved that.

But it was her zest for life and how she managed to design her own special environment according to her rules that was most admirable. Albeit, the day she truly became my role-model and changed my life forever was the day she exposed her personal pain and vulnerability, by sharing when her youthful heart was broken in an effort to help me get past my latest heartbreaking saga.

With tears pouring down my face, she sat me down, tenderly held my hand, and began to tell her story.

"Darling, when I was about your age I went to this glamorous party in Manhattan, where I met this very handsome photographer. He instantly 'fell in love' with my smile and proceeded to hire me on the spot to be *the*

Face for a series of new skincare ads. It should have been the most exciting time of my life, but it was marred by my obsession of wanting him to fall in love with all of me, not just my face. I was so crushed and devastated when he threw me over for the next 'It Girl.'

One day my adored "big sister" friend Sonia came home from work and found me crying on her front steps. "What's wrong?" with great concern she asked.

Through my sobs she managed to decipher that my heart had been 'irreparably' broken, and I felt rejected and unlovable. With sympathetic eyes from a woman who has known those feelings herself, she sat down and put her arm around me and with a sigh began to speak.

"Ketsy, I want to play a little game with you, so please indulge me, OK?" She continued.

I weakly nodded yes.

"As I begin," she said, "you must willingly surrender any assumptions and presumed conclusions as to what you believe are so and what isn't so."

I tearfully nodded ok.

"Next, instruct your logical mind to slow down just long enough to cross into the world of imagination. See yourself fearlessly running past all of the reality checks and mental obstacles, while ignoring the voices saying, "Sonia has officially gone crazy!"

A quivering smile curled my lips at her perception.

"Close your eyes and focus on your perfect love and *listen* to the heartfelt apology for taking so long to finally get to you. Note the *feelings* of compassion you feel for all the difficulties that had to be overcome, the never-ending efforts put on things to be improved and the guilt felt from all the mistakes made. Acknowledge all the acceptance and admiration for a beautiful smile, loving nature, special qualities and attributes. Enjoy the delight in the approval and appreciation of your perfect body and unique way of being. Observe the feelings of peace and deep satisfaction in finally being fully seen, completely loved, safe and secure."

So, I closed my eyes, took three big deep breaths and slowly began the journey from here to there. After what felt like quite a while, I opened my eyes and nodded my head, yes. *Yes,* I felt the presence of this great love. She gave me a big smile and continued.

"And finally the last and most important step, that if followed, I promise will bring you real true love. Are you ready?"

I slowly nodded in agreement.

"Take all those feelings of love and acceptance and give them to the person who deserves them the most -- YOU! From this moment forth, make *You* the great love of your life. Saturate *Your* essence with sensations of joy, passion, enthusiasm and pure delight! Treat *You* like the most important person in the entire world by giving *You* the things that you are always seeking from another; the symbolic proof that *You are truly loved.*"

She continued, "Buy *Yourself* flowers to wake-up to everyday. Spoil *You* with *Your* favorite treats, fruits, beverages and all the very best ingredients to make a delicious dinner at a candlelit set table. Then sit down and savor every bite. Those love songs you listen to? Sing them to *You*! Most importantly, start now and never stop, to speak to *yourself* as you would to someone you really love and adore.

Once you truly love yourself for the amazing one-of-a-kind work of art that you are, the inner glow flowing out of you will beam 'Scotty' right to you! Accept that you can't change the past but you can change how you chose to perceive it. Figure out whether you are going to love yourself completely today, as is, or hate yourself forever more, the choice is yours!"

This amazing woman who gave me life, shared her secret for being one of the happiest and really one of the most beautiful women in the world: be a woman who had absolute self-confidence derived from being *Madly in Love with Yourself*! Her magnetic personality and irresistible glow came from truly loving and respectfully taking care of her well-being. She understood the great blessing that came with being a child of God. What a gift to give any child -- what a gift to give to yourself.

En-JOY!

"Our deepest fear is not that we are inadequate.
Our deepest fear is that we are powerful beyond measure. It is our light, not our darkness that most frightens us.

We ask ourselves...'Who am I to be brilliant, gorgeous, talented, fabulous?' Actually, who are you not to be?
You are a child of God. Your playing small does not serve the world.

As you let your own light shine, you unconsciously give other people permission to do the same. As you are liberated from your own fear, your presence automatically liberates others."

Marianne Williamson

HOW TO LOVE YOURSELF WHEN YOU NEED IT THE MOST!

A "Guided" Exercise sent from above...

"Why are you trying so hard to fit in when you were born to stand out?"

Ian Wallace

Every now and then *the best of us* have days or nights when for whatever reason we feel less *than our best* because of one reason or another. More often than not, those black moods come rolling in when the only one around to make you feel better is you. Finding your way out of the dark clouds to the bright sunshine of feeling loved and worthy can sometimes feel almost impossible.

So when I was in that exact place just days ago, feeling frustrated about having so much more to do to meet my deadline, while dealing with a serious bout of writer's block, "this evolved master" felt like a little lost puppy in search of a big dish of some good old-fashion loving, where there was none in sight.

I know these feelings only too well, not only from my own experiences, but from having the opportunity to revisit a version of these emotions with thousands of men and women around the world. The bottom-line question is always the same; "What can I do to get back to feeling positive and excited, when now things seem so dismal and difficult?"

Intellectually I knew that this would pass and that my feelings about my obstacles didn't define me. Because I wasn't looking for an excuse to take my foot off "the petal" to slow down a bit, it was obvious that I needed an attitude adjustment, *right now*, Big Time!

So I closed down my BFF computer and took myself outside for a well-needed breath of fresh air. As I was standing on the deck taking in deep breaths and the beauty of the day, something drew my eyes up beyond the flowers, beyond the plants and trees toward the late day sun. As I stared into the bright light I started to hear that voice again, whispering in my head and directing me *to "remember something that you've done that you are most proud of, and then describe how you felt when that experience was happening."*

I really can't say for sure where "the voice" is coming from, but being one that does believe in magic and miracles, I slowly began to acquiesce to the request by responding in a rout fashion and doing what I was asked to do. I went back to a time in my life when I felt I had accomplished something that almost everyone who knew me, including me, felt was almost impossible.

Even though I kept moving forward and doing what turned out to be one right action after another, when it all came together, I was as much in awe as everyone else that I had actually pulled it off!

It wasn't one exact moment in time that I returned to that revitalized my sense of worth, it was more of an all-over amazement and delight that I had actually done what I said I was going to do! Remembering this was just what I needed to get back on course.

Just this brief visit to one of my peak experiences, (again, thank you Abraham Maslow for your brilliant work) I noticed my energy shifting. The more I indulged in memories of my achievements with pride and joy, the better I felt. This metaphoric "humongous hug, umpteen pats on the back and standing ovation" was just what the doctor ordered! It was a *huge* wake-up call to the damaging effects of making future endeavors the yard stick to your present day happiness and well-being. This project was just one more in a long list of past and future endeavors, and to let any part of this process diminish my efforts in any way, would be a big mistake. Talk about a V-8 moment.

It was as if I had been lead into this experience to reawaken my personal power and inner wisdom by some sort of *"Guide"* that is there to protect me from myself. This might sound crazy, especially since I don't often look to "angels or guides" for help. I tend to go right to The Source. But I can't think of any other explanation as I really did feel guided on this journey!

As brightly as the sun was shining that day, is the brilliance of the message I am now sharing with you. Every now and then you must stop running ahead and take a minute to remember and ruminate over all of the hurdles and challenges you've had to overcome to get to where you are today. Even if today doesn't feel like your best, those events are what got you to where you are, and today's actions will take you to where you are going.

Now is the time to recall some of your finest moments to get your engine roaring and reenergizing yourself. Find as many as you can and then use those *high five* moments to send an electric current of validation throughout your whole body. By returning to good memories long ago put on the back burner, you will feel as if you are riding the road of life with more cylinders than the Bugatti Veyron 16.4 Super Sport!

But this *guided exercise* wasn't over yet. After feeling completely buoyant, I sat down and within minutes another form of "spirited" questioning popped into my head. This one asked the Joy of twenty-five years ago ....that I know and remember quite well... '*What achievements, qualities and characteristics would you have hoped and wanted the JOY of today to possess?*'

I loved this question. As I repeated back the responses in a question/ answer mode, this wonderful sensation started to flood my body. Almost as if my insides were being affectionately massaged. I can only imagine that these feelings were generated from the effervescent accolades that I was allowing myself to joyfully accept from myself to myself!

To think back on what my goals and aspirations were so many decades ago, and then to see that I had not only embodied the qualities and characteristics I admired, but even some outstanding ones that weren't even on my viewfinder~ was a totally awesome feeling! No lies, no BS, no need to make anything up to make myself feel bigger, better or more important. I just honestly looked over my life, told my truth, and it was great!

Without having some sort of local, national or world presence for doing something "so amazing," every single one of you has done things in your life that deserves a standing ovation. Whether anyone else knows about it, agrees or sees it, doesn't matter. What matters is that *just the thought* of what you did brings you pride and great satisfaction.

When you give yourself a the gift of remembering and reliving the noteworthy moments of your life, it will feel as if you've been shot up with some sort of high octane fuel. As soon as the jets are fired up, they will burn off your limiting thoughts and within minutes you'll be back on your winning game!

Learning the art of *Loving Yourself When You Need it The Most* is a necessary skill we all need to cultivate more. As Max Muller said, "A flower cannot blossom without sunshine, and man cannot live without love." So easily we build others up with our love and support while beating ourselves down with the whips of our perceived flaws, faults and limitations. Not good.

LIFE ~ LUST ~ and **LOVE**...

But as we all know too well, you will never be the best at your work, your passions or capable of fully loving someone else, until you truly love yourself first.

This *Guided* Exercise in remembering who I am by loving myself (I am sticking with this theory until someone proves me wrong), was an amazing way to readjust my attitude and realign all my senses so that they support my highest good and greatest intentions. Trust me when I say...try it, you'll like it!

En-JOY!

"At age 20, we worry about what others think of us. At age 40, we don't care what they think of us. At age 60, we discover they haven't been thinking of us at all!"

Ann Landers

AGING

What is so marvelous about this quote is that most of us have had the good fortune to have experienced at least two of these ages, if not all three. So we know just how true these words really are. But if you were to ask "the know it all" 20 year olds if they are looking forward to being a "fabulous wise confident 60 year old," their probable answer would be "Hell, no!"

The guru of advice columnist Ann Landers words reminds us that as we become more experienced we tend to move away from the egocentric concerns of youth to the more realistic perceptions of more mature adults. We come to realize that we are not the center of the universe, and that's a good thing. As a result," the more seasoned" are now free to do what they want when they want, not constrained by what is construed to be the good opinions of others.

If you truly want to experience an Extraordinary life, it's essential to embrace all the advantages that come with getting older, opposed to resenting what is so. If you really want to know how to age successfully, getting advice from others you respect for how well they are aging in all respects is a brilliant idea.

So congrats on getting this book!

But before you go any further or delve deeper into my secret memoirs, I want you to stop for a moment and ask yourself: *How old would you be if you didn't know how old you were?"*

Once you have answered that truthfully, ask yourself an even more important question...*How closely does the life you are living now resemble how someone that age would be living?*

If close great! If not so close, maybe now is the time to read some stories that just might help you reverse the clock.

En-JOY!

"In terms of days and moments lived, you'll never again be as young as you are right now, so spend this day, the youth of your future, in a way that deflects regret. Invest in yourself. Have some fun. Do something important. Love somebody extra. In one sense, you're just a kid, but a kid with enough years on her to know that every day is priceless."

Victoria Moran

HOW TO FEEL AGELESS FOR DECADES!

"To love oneself is the beginning of a lifelong romance" Oscar Wilde

I've thought and I've thought, and you know, I can't remember a time in my life when age wasn't an issue. It seems like *forever* I have been either too young to do this or too old to do that. "No, Joy, you can't go where we're going. You're too young, and you're old enough to know better! Or, "don't you think you're too young to go to a place like that, dressed like that?" Then what seems like a blink of an eye, I was asked "aren't you too old to go to a place like that, dressed like that?" Geez!

For so many years I would go on interviews for one thing or another and was told that I didn't have enough experience (I was too young), then suddenly one day I was being told that I was "over-qualified" (do I dare say too old?) Then there is my all-time favorite which I have heard my entire life, "Act your age." Yet after all these years I still can't find an instruction manual on what that is supposed to look like!

But now that I have become a woman of "a certain age," which as far as I can see I have always been of a certain age but apparently now it's something I should be concerned about, I am on a mission to blur the lines.

To start with, everywhere I look there is yet another piece done in a magazine, book, television or radio show where another "expert" is determined to do whatever they can to make sure no one is living in some blissful youth fantasy. Each one seems designed to inform you of another potential problem lurking around the corner, just waiting to take you down. Then, they benevolently proceed to share the perfect diet, vitamins and exercise programs, skin care products or unlimited forms of multiple procedures that guarantee an "anti-aging" life.

As the saying goes,' I don't know if it is good and I don't know if it's bad,' but what I do know is that over the last three months I have been to at least six different gatherings with women between 35 and 75, where at some point in the evening the discussion got around to the issues of aging. Even though I felt as if I had this issue under control, I couldn't help noticing how these evenings left me feeling a bit disheartened. Especially since I have always felt that if God is really good to me, getting older would be one of the perks!

It finally dawned on me that if I didn't find some way to truly embrace the aging process and all the inevitable changes that come with it, I sure as heck was going to have a pretty miserable time over the next forty years. And, if it wasn't miserable, it certainly would be a far cry from Extraordinary!
So I went on a search for some answers on how to age youthfully with style and grace. The perfect answer came from my special friend Sheila, a huge advocate for celebrating the age you are fortunate enough to now

be. "To appreciate all the gifts and life lessons this age has given you is one of the secrets to fully enjoying life."

She shared with me the story of just recently going out to dinner with a really cute guy when in cocktail conversation she discovered that they had gone to the same high school, except he graduated ten years earlier! So there she was, an advocate for honoring your age, yet questioning herself on how she was going to get around that bit of factoid. When suddenly a discussion she just recently had with a very savvy and wise friend popped into her head.

"As our lunch date was coming to an end, it began to rain cats and dogs and of course I immediately started to complain about how it was going to ruin my shoes, my day, my plans, etc., etc. Typical of Martin, he calmly looked at me and said, '*Sheila, choose the rain.*'

'*Choose the rain, how can I choose the rain? I don't even have an umbrella!*' Sheila said she shouted back.

He looked at me lovingly and said, '*Is the rain going to stop because you want it to? Is it going to just go away? Why not choose to accept it, see the beauty and all the gifts that come with the rain and let it add to your day instead of diminishing it.*"

OMG, there it was, the answer written across the sky! If she could choose to be in the moment *exactly as it was*, while at the same time being grateful for all the wondrous things that come with that moment, her experiences could be totally different and much better!

As Sheila remembered Martin's brilliant words, she turned to her fella and proudly announced that she had graduated ten years earlier. He thought that was cool, had no problem with it, and proceeded to ask her out for next Saturday night. As Henry David Thoreau said, *"It's not what you look at that matters, it's what you see."*

So, there it was and here it is now, the ultimate non-surgical way to absolutely age youthfully for decades that has pass the test of time. A solution so true and so right-on, a directive as effective now as when I wrote about it over a decade ago: *Choose the Rain. Choose what is unchangeable,* what is so, and then find your own way to include and embrace it all in a way that will support you being the best and living your best life ever!

My attitude and personal inspiration on aging came from a fabulous quote that I read many years ago from an interview with the French actress Simone Signoret.

She told the reporter that when she died she'd be very young.

"*Really,*" said the reporter, "*at what age do you think you will die?*"

"*Oh, I don't know,*" said Ms. Signoret, "*Maybe 85 or 95. But when I die, I will be very, very young.*"

Everything, and I do mean *everything,* boils down to your attitude and perception. Once you can appreciate the mileage that's been accumulated on this amazing machine called your body and then truly acknowledge the gift of each additional year, every extra minute will be perceived as a blessing not a curse.

"The trick is in what you emphasize. You either make yourself miserable or you make yourself happy. The amount of work is all the same." If you can *Choose The Rain* as joyfully as you *choose* the sunshine, if you can *choose* to embrace all of the aging process as joyfully as you *choose* to embrace the knowledge and wisdom you've gained along the way...a bit of maturity can be a very sexy thing. Not to mention an admired accessory to be worn with panache, pride and exuberant JOY!

En-JOY!

"To keep the heart unwrinkled, to be hopeful, kindly, cheerful, reverent...that is to triumph over old age."

Thomas Bailey Aldrich

AGELESS BEAUTY

"There is a fountain of youth: It's in your mind, your talents, the creativity you bring to your life and the lives of the people you love. When you learn to tap this source, you will truly have defeated age."

This quote, attributed to Sophia Loren, is *exactly* how I feel about how to defeat age as our culture sees it! That is why I knew I would be remiss if I didn't properly introduce my beloved audience to one of my greatest role-models for aging with style and grace, the truly quintessential ideal of sensuality, sexuality, femininity and true phenomenal womanliness. The soul of elegance and timeless beauty who's still rocking it at the ripe young age of 79, as of this writing, and who I want to be like when I grow up!

Considered one of the last living goddesses, with her wonderful laugh, sensuous walk, often noted volatile passions with a magnanimous spirit and a witty quick intelligence, are just some of the things that make her so irresistible. In fact, I recently read that at the end of a dinner party with high-powered players in Hollywood, all the men lined up like little boys waiting to have their pictures taken with "the charming, beautiful and funny

Sophia." With these kinds of lasting credentials, emulating a woman like Sophia Loren sure seems like a smart thing to do. Which to the best of my ability in my own version, I've been trying to do for years.

What I have learned from studying these *Sheros's* is that being an ageless beauty has very little to do with the perfection of any body part or having a flawless canvas that is wrapped in a designer's high ticket whatever, but has *everything to* do with the life you put into your life!

It's about having a *joie de vivre* that's contagious. A way of being that lifts the spirits of all mankind and nature's animals. A particular quality that is intangible, something you can't quite put your finger on, yet when you see it, it's unforgettable. It's the mystery behind the glossy exterior that makes women captivating enigmas.

"Beauty is how you feel inside, and it reflects in your eyes. It is not something physical. Sex appeal is fifty percent what you've got and fifty percent what people think you've got. I think the quality of sexiness comes from within. It is something that is in you or it isn't and it really doesn't have much to do with breasts or thighs or the pout of your lips.

After all these years, I am still involved in the process of self-discovery. It's better to explore life and make mistakes than to play it safe. Mistakes are part of the dues one pays for a full life, and having a full life is what matters the most." This is just a small sampling of *the wisdom of Sophia* that I've used to guide me forward.

Thanks to my girl "SoLo" and many other great women, the expression *true beauty is ageless* is finally being acknowledged and appreciated. Many women in their 60's and 70's have proven to be the accepted standard for desirable women, which is fabulous news for gals in their 40's and 50's. Because if you are blessed and lucky, you will be one of those ages before you know it!

"The seasoned woman is spicy. She's been marinated in experience." Proof of that pudding is seeing Jessica Lange at age 65, Helen Mirren at age 69, and drum roll here please, Katherine Deneuve at age 71 being hired to be The Face of major cosmetic and product companies! These women and many others over 40 are living proof that the accepted and embraced new standard for being attractive, sensuous and beautiful is the more seasoned sophisticated woman.

"Sex appeal doesn't go away because we don't have such a precise definition of beauty. Quirkiness and charm are more valued than some static idea of perfection. In the United States, beauty is almost mathematical and can only be achieved in your 20s. Aging is rather an American fear—a young country afraid to get old. Here, buildings are old and forever beautiful" says Laurence Vely, an editor at Vanity Fair France, who feels most women become more attractive with age...and wisdom.

Once you hit 40, you finally begin to know yourself and what suits you. [You] have real confidence."

Since I totally agree with this Frenchman, I think it is time to share a few more of this savvy woman's insider secrets for being an ageless beauty. Number one is....

1. *Always Consider Yourself an Ageless Beauty no matter what your age.* Believing that you can be an object of love and desire, no matter what your age, determines how you act and respond to circumstances. Your behavior reflects back the way others see and treat you, especially when you're confident. Just don't make the mistake of pretending you are forever Twenty-five.

For the record, it's been proven that when you have a positive attitude toward aging long before you really "begin to age," you will age better. When you have an affirming belief in yourself, a favorable attitude about the world in general and appreciate the little things in life with a positive approach to the future, it's been proven to increase your life span on an average of seven and a half years!"

2. *Exhibit your self-reliance.* It's extremely appealing when others sense that your choices come from trusting that you know you can handle almost any unknown circumstance that is thrown your way. Staying calm while not letting your feathers get ruffled shows a woman independent of the opinion or approval of others...or their material possessions. Add generosity, and this attitude is extremely attractive at any age.

3. *Inhabit your body completely.* Every shape has its unique curves and delights, and a woman who knows how to display them just plain rocks! Displaying your authentic confidence by the way you move your body, not simply in bed, in everything you do. Make it your signature, whether perky and energetic or possibly languorous and full of grace. When you include your eyes and mouth ~ it causes spontaneous combustion! So much is conveyed in your movements.

4. *Adapt the sounds of a cultivated voice*, as it is something which only grows more alluring with age. A resonant modulated voice, opposed to one that is high and squeaky, is so much more engaging. A woman who has control over the tone and the inflection, plus the colors, can float you on the waves of her voice. Add an unguarded laughter that comes easily and often with a slight lilt, and you become very intriguing.

5. *Use your refined experienced mind* to become an interested and interesting woman. Use your years of experience and observations to create the context of conversational stories. Mastery over the fine art of communications is a skill well worth the effort. Knowing when to get excited and when to slow down, when to submit and when to hold-back, is a talent to cultivate, as it "lights up" everything.

6. *Create your own unique style*. A woman that understands what works for her, what flatters her, what makes her style unique, often above and beyond trends, shows self-awareness and that is very appealing.

An ageless beauty comfortably shows all her various personalities; powerful, sensual, confident, soft and approachable, in her own particular fashion.

7. *Be Adventurous* and give yourself permission to fully embrace and enjoy all the moments of your day. Let your JOY become like honey to the bees and flowers to the butterflies. A great love for life combined with a constant curiosity and desire to learn and grow keeps you mentally and physically young so you can to enjoy all the many enticing ways there are to enjoy life. But whatever you do, above all, have a hell of a good time!

8. *Smile a lot and Laugh easily* about almost everything if you truly want to look and feel ageless! Every single time you smile you are giving yourself a natural facelift by pulling all your muscles up and pumping up all kinds of feel-good endorphins through your body for optimal good health plus an unmatchable glow.

Add laughter and you've added mini workouts that burn calories and works the abs. Laughter also helps blood flow, lowers blood sugar levels, reduces stress, improves sleep and raises the level of fighting antibodies in the body, which also helps to boost your immune system. Just that thought makes me feel youthful and that is definitely worth smiling about!

En-JOY!

"Perhaps we shall learn, as we pass through this age, that the 'other self" is more powerful than the physical self we see when we look into a mirror."

Napoleon Hill

OWN YOUR MAGNIFICENCE: How to Light up Every Room!

"A bird doesn't sing because it has an answer, it sings because it has a song."

   Not long ago the amazing Dr. Maya Angelo passed away leaving a legacy of words and actions that still continue to inspire us to find the courage to figure out who we really are and who we really want to be. It took a re-reading of her marvelous poem called *Phenomenal Woman* to reignite my memories of another amazing woman who first taught me how to take ownership of my own magnificence.

"Pretty women wonder where my secret lies.
I'm not cute or built to suit a fashion model's size.
But when I start to tell them, they think I'm telling lies.
I say...

It's in the reach of my arms. The span of my hips,
The stride of my step, the curl of my lips.
It's the fire in my eyes, and the flash of my teeth,
The swing in my waist and the joy in my feet.

I'm a woman. Phenomenally.
Phenomenal woman. That's me.

*Men themselves have wondered...What they see in me.
They try so much...But they can't touch my inner
mystery. When I try to show them, they say they still
can't see. I say, It's in the arch of my back, the sun of
my smile, The ride of my breasts, the grace of my style.
It's in the click of my heels, the bend of my hair,
the palm of my hand, the need for my care.*

*I'm a woman Phenomenally.
Phenomenal woman. That's me."*

Years ago when I was a professional photographer I
had the pleasure of photographing Ma Mère, a fabulous
American-born woman who had moved to Paris at the
ripe old age of twenty because she adored everything
French! After years of being a top model, stylist and
beloved wife of an apparently adoring (deceased)
husband, she is now in New York living a grand life
to its fullest.

To this day I don't know what possessed Ma Mère to
take me under her wing, but her shared secret has taken
me to places women far more beautiful, accomplished,
brilliant, wealthy and successful have only dreamed of
going. I say secret, opposed to secrets, because *everything* she ever said comes back to the most important
lesson any woman or man can ever learn: *How to Own
Your Magnificence.*

In a hundred different ways she encouraged me to
love every single part of myself so that there would
never be any doubt of my own self-confidence, self-
worth or self-respect for whatever you choose to do

and wherever you need to go, were absolute. While other young women were being educated in the great value of mastering domestic skills and the various ways to accommodate others, I was being taught to embrace my own feminine power, while always taking full responsibility for my mind, body, spirit experiences.

This jewel of a woman taught me the importance of only listening to the thoughts that empower and serve you, while consciously being on-guard to eradicate and eliminate any negative ones, no matter from whence they came." Never let anyone or anything get in the way of loving your one-of-a-kind sparkling unique self!"

I can still see Ma Mère sitting in her bountiful garden, captivating and mesmerizing me with all her fascinating stories that she skillfully weaved her words of wisdom throughout. As one does with colorful threads woven through a substantial fabric, she would then proceed to create a beautiful needlepoint design of my life. Slowly, she would begin again to teach her little mentee this very important life lesson.

"*Mon chéri*, if you want to be the kind of rare jewel worthy of love, adoration and special care, you must develop ownership of *Your Own Magnificence* and that can only be generated from the inside out. The depth and strength of one's own inner light is what makes a woman truly beautiful.

When the outside begins to change, possibly not so much to your liking, which happens eventually to all of us, others will barely notice. The brightness that comes from your inner wisdom and the love you have for life and yourself will diffuse any so called flaws. This alone will make you fascinating and unforgettable. Like an expensive bottle of French parfum you will be cherished and intoxicating!"

Ma Mère was one of the most exciting women I have ever known and those qualities never diminished. Men and women of all ages were enamored by her magnetic charm and the ageless beauty she wore like the finest cashmere scarf. She had great respect for the natural gifts she had been given at birth and she embellished them with adornment as naturally as breathing. She never understood why anyone would *poubelle leur temple,* trash the temple that carries their soul.

"How could anyone have such little respect for the body that their Creator has given them for the most incredible ride of their life? *C'est fou,* it's crazy." She totally believed in the idea of polishing the outer stone so that your physical presence always had the luster of a top grade jewel. Focusing on your inner gifts and always listening to your intuition was what she believed made every woman her own priceless work of art.

When you *Own Your Magnificence,* you are in the light, owning your perfection without any false pride or arrogance. Simply knowing how special you really are and that any man or woman, lover or friend is lucky to have you in their life.

Some of the best advice my adored Ma Mère gave me was to never forget that, unequivocally, nothing is more appealing than a self-assured self-confident woman. She would always say...

"You must always be *à l'aise dans votre peau*.... comfortable in your own skin, and never ever be an imitation of anyone but yourself. The world needs authentic beings with the courage to be who they truly are. When you can *Own Your Magnificence* you send out an indefinable energy that will make you light up every space you walk into, everywhere you go. You become like the Eiffel Tower light show in Paris at midnight on New Year's Eve: unforgettably electrifying."

En-JOY!

"Find joy in everything you choose to do. Every job, relationship, home... it's your responsibility to love it, or change it."

Chuck Palahniuk

JOY ~ JOY ~ JOY

"Joy is to fun what the deep sea is to a puddle... It's a feeling inside that can hardly be contained." Terry Pratchett

Recently while attending a TEDx event, I was given the distinct pleasure of being able to speak in front of a large audience for just 30 seconds on a topic that I was informed of only one minute before I went on the stage: *Tell us about the first time you fell in love.* With literally less than a minute to figure out what to say, I was on the stage speaking my truth.

"I fell in love for the very first time when I won the lottery"...a two second pause with a now wide-eyed audience staring back at me, I went on..."the day I was named JOY." Smiles began to pop up all over the room as I continued.

"I've known forever that I was sent into this world blessed with 'the assignment' of spreading the feelings of JOY whenever and wherever I could, instead of "the job" of having to inspire empathy or compassion by exhibiting a very difficult hard life. Because I know deep in my being that *I Am the Source* of Life showing up as *JOY,* and by doing that I make a difference in the world, I fell in love, and have been in love with JOY ever since."

211

JOY was and is my first great love, so speaking my truth, as always, worked out just perfectly. I have always believed that if you've been glorified with the name Joy, that you have some sort of responsibility to live a JOY-filled life. And though I know there isn't any definitive guaranteed answer for having an Extraordinary life, what I do know for sure, is that the absence of deeply felt JOY will pretty much guarantee a life far less than spectacular.

JOY, the source of great pleasure or delight, is one of the greatest human emotions that you can experience. It goes way beyond any happiness that can be felt by obtaining a new possession, seeing your hard work finally pay off, or a sense of relief from daily stress and anxiety. It is much deeper a feeling than satisfaction, pleasure or happiness.

JOY is a quality of thought that infuses your mind, body and spirit with a deep sense of personal power, inner wisdom and heightened mental clarity. It can stimulate your immune system, can increase your energy and help you stretch beyond any previously assumed boundaries.

JOY opens your heart, helps you stay centered in the midst of your difficulties and enhances your ability to tap into your unlimited creativity, infinite possibilities and wisdom. This amazing state of mind manifests itself in your daily life in just a heartbeat, as more freedom, love, passion, enthusiasm, excitement, peace and harmony.

Pretty incredible this feeling called JOY, don't you think?

As crazy as it may seem, there are actually people who are afraid of being *too* positive, *too* successful or having *too* much JOY in their lives. They have unfortunately chosen to believe at some deeper level that they just don't deserve *too* much of a good thing. Mentally and physically agreeing to live a life filled with continuous self-fulfilled prophecies, which includes suffering, pain and disappointments, instead of choosing to envision an easier and more JOY-filled life.

JOY is an emotion that many people say they really want to experience but even so, as Dr. Brené Brown states, "it often brings with it a feeling of terror." Admitting that there's a very tricky element involved with this rare emotion. "If you were to ask me what's the most terrifying, difficult emotion we feel as humans," she says, "I would say JOY."

Calling JOY "terrifying" may seem strange, but Dr. Brown explains that the fear stems from having your JOY taken away.

"How many of you have ever sat up and thought, 'Wow, work's going really well, good relationship with my partner, kids and parents seem to be doing okay.' Then in the next moment you think, 'Holy crap. Something bad is going to happen.'"

She then asked her audience. "You know what that is? [It's] when we have lost our tolerance for being so vulnerable. JOY becomes foreboding: 'I'm scared it's

going to be taken away. The other shoe's going to drop...'
What we do in moments of joyfulness is try to beat
vulnerability to the punch."

She goes on to say that she has never interviewed
a single person who talks about the capacity to really
experience and soften into JOY who doesn't actively
practice gratitude. Truly joyful people do not allow
fear to take away from fully experiencing JOY. They
don't say, 'There's a shudder of terror about feeling
joyful. I'm going to dress-rehearse tragedy," she says.
"They say, 'I'm going to practice gratitude... Gratitude
is a practice. It is tangible.'"

But it isn't just gratitude that's been found to have
such positive effects. It is many emotions, including
learned optimism, generosity, and hopefulness.

In fact, a three-to-one ratio of positive to negative
emotions can create a life of flourishing JOY. Much
research backs the belief that when you think positive
thoughts — about gratitude, optimism, kindness and
JOY~ you activate our left prefrontal cortex and flood
your body with feel-good hormones! Beside the benefit
of a good mood in the short run, as noted before, it
strengthens your immune system in the long run.
JOY is just plain simply good for your health!

Now on the other side, literally, when you think
negative, angry, worried, hopeless and pessimistic
thoughts, you activate your right prefrontal cortex
and flood your body with stress hormones. This can
send you into fight or flight mode and a state of

depression that suppresses your immune system. In other words, you are immersing your body, mind and spirit in good or bad chemicals based on the thoughts that *only you* have complete control over! Something to think about, don't you think?

I've known for quite a while that we are all responsible for our thoughts and how they affected our mental and emotional health. But it wasn't until I began to study the work of Doctor Abraham Maslow, the creator of Human Potential Psychology that I really began to understand how dramatically my thoughts could affect my physical health and stamina.

Dr. Maslow's work discovered that happy healthy "actualized" individuals have the ability to mentally return to past peak experiences and the sensations they felt when experiencing those events. They then were able to use those remembered feelings of great enthusiasm, delight and JOY, as a stimulus to create more JOY-filled moments in the present that ultimately affected the quality of their lives.

So my first step was to start from where I was with what I had. I firmly believed that it would be more than enough to lead me into a life that was even bigger and better. I declared to the universe, "that I am now willing and able to let go of all my limiting beliefs and ready to learn all my lessons through JOY. No longer will I wait for the perfect person or conditions to bring forth what I need to become the woman I want to be."

My Second Step was to assume ownership of what I know to be my life purpose; to inspire, motivate and teach others to fully embrace the power of JOY.

Once I started to see the results that others were experiencing from the message I was sharing around the "magic" of THE FORMULA for turning anything ordinary into everything Extraordinary, it no longer matter if I was speaking to one person or a group of a thousand personally and professionally. Whether I was mentoring an individual or consulting with an entire corporate office on better communication, I made JOY my highest commitment, and the quality of my life changed in ways I never could have imagined!

Finding your source of JOY, *right now,* is the most important work you will ever do...that is if having the best that life can offer has any appeal to you.

What I know for sure, is that once you decide to make JOY your highest commitment, then truly *everything* begins to bring you JOY, *even if* it's only being aware that in the worst of times there will be another gift for your personal growth if you just stay your course.

As Joseph Campbell said, "Find a place inside where there's joy, and the joy will burn out the pain." When you take the time to find that place and allow it to burn brightly, the very littlest things and most insignificant moments become another reason for your happiness and JOY. Once you can do this, it's amazing how quickly the big and very significant things start to appear almost everywhere. It's really quite Extraordinary!

The challenge is to notice where and when any of your emotions are mired in any negative or fearful thoughts, especially when those feelings are about some unknown or unrealized expectation that could possibly happen in the future. This is where reframing is a magical tool!

Here are a few of my tried and true tips for filling yourself up with pure JOY that I guarantee if taken to heart will show you an Extraordinary life you might only have dreamed was possible for yourself.

"JOY is prayer; JOY is strength: JOY is love; JOY is a net of love by which you can catch souls."

1. *To paraphrase my earlier message....*

Step one...Start from where you are with just what you have, holding to the belief that it will be more than enough to lead you into something bigger and better. *Step two*...Take full ownership of what you feel to be your calling and live from that truth. *Step three* ... Become consciously aware of all of your thoughts, especially when you're worried about something that you think could happen negatively in the future. Then begin to reframe them to serve you and bring you JOY. *Step four*... Learn to Relax and Trust. Believe that you are blessed and everything will work out in your favor.

2. *Begin & End the Day with JOYful Thoughts*

When you first open your eyes, before you even get out of bed, spend at least five minutes thinking about things that you are grateful for and imagine things that could possibly bring you JOY today.

217

Think about the smallest daily pleasure, as well as the biggest and most impossible possibilities that could happen in your life today. Focus your thoughts on how good that feels. Then spend the rest of the day with your eyes wide open looking for proof!

JOY can come from anything and is everywhere, but you have to choose JOY and keep choosing it every day. Experiencing JOY, like everything else, is *always* mind over matter. But so worth the effort!

Happiness is a delightful emotion. It can be generated from a feeling about some momentary occurrence, a recent achievement or instant gratification from some attainment or a sense of satisfaction. But JOY, JOY goes deep into you're your body and mind, and settles even deeper in your heart. It is embedded in the spirit of the soul that permeates all of your being.

That is why is *so important Not* to begin your day with any negative or upsetting thoughts dancing in your head. It's been said that for every minute you are angry, you loss sixty seconds of happiness and JOY! What a waste, can you imagine? So start today and jump out of bed with JOY! It's a great exercise and an excellent way to begin to have a truly JOY-filled day and life!

When you day is done and you are about to "dormir con los angelitas"~go to sleep with the angels~ take five minutes to think *only* positive thoughts about the day and plans for your future desires. Never go to bed at night with negative angry thoughts, as they will settle into your being and cause havoc with your health.

3. *Become Passionate About Everything!*

   Passion is an intense emotion that when you use it properly can intensify any intangible obstacles, such as time or energy. It can turn work into play, a mere human being into a God or Goddess and a simple event into a marvelous occasion. Since passion and desire go hand in hand, using this combination to manifest your heart's desire can become one of the most powerful means for creating continuously JOY throughout your life. It's been called the "magic elixir" for making a person better at everything they do.

   The specific kind of passion I am referring to isn't the all-consuming lustful feeling that overtakes our loins and senses, but an emotion that goes much deeper and encompasses a broader range of feelings and thoughts. It can be for something that may seem insignificant in the big picture, such as the handmade chocolate truffles at Morton's Market, or as life changing as meeting the love of your life or realizing various forms of your work being embraced by millions of people around the world. (Hmmm, I wonder whose desire that could be?)

   All I know is that when your body is filled with feelings of pure passion for whatever, it's like the glowing waters from the bioluminescent bay flooding every single pore of your being that sends out a light that attracts all kinds of incredible people and opportunities.

   To actualize your special calling requires finding and pursuing your passion. The dream and the dreamer are always matched and the ways and means to realize your greatest dreams are all around you, once you find and follow your passion. All it takes is to keep your eyes and heart open to your feelings and following your North Star; 4 steps forward, 2 steps back, 9 steps forward, 3 steps back, 12 forward, 2 steps back, a little to the right and a little to the left, etc. Then low and behold there you are; smacked dab in the middle of your wildest dream! That place you've been searching for to find true peace and JOY, the meaning and reason for your beautiful life.

4. *DANCE...*

Did you know dancing with a JOY-filled spirit literally builds new brain cells? And that new brain cells can *only* grow once you're totally focused and excited about an activity? "When done with a self-initiated movement, exploration, interaction and physical experience for the JOY and challenge of it, you will facilitate neurogenesis (nerve growth) for a lifetime." Which means when you give energy and passion to anything that offers a great mix of challenges it can bring you more JOY!

'It is music and dance that make me at peace with the world...at peace with myself," Nelson Mandela said at his 92nd birthday party when he stood up dancing rhythmic steps and occasionally punching the air with joy. His "dance for JOY" has since been named The Strut, as it's meant to represent shaking the burdens of life off your shoulder in a victory of the human spirit, and it is emulated all across South Africa by dancers of all races and ages.

Even though I never quite put it that way, when there is music and I get to dance, my mind, body and spirit are filled with happiness and pure JOY. I feel as if something has comes over me and I am connected to the universe and all is right in the world. If you are not a dancer try it with those thoughts in mind. Don't worry about who is watching and what they are thinking. At some point what others think is none of your business. Especially if being filled with JOY is your end goal.

As the Japanese proverb goes, *"We're fools whether we dance or not, so we might as well dance!"*

5. *Live in a state of Conscious Awareness...*

Nevel Goddard said that, "health, wealth, beauty and genius are not created, they are manifested by the arrangement of your mind...by your concept of yourself, a concept that you will accept and consent to be the truth." When you make it a practice to live your life in awareness of your thoughts and actions, you've taken full control of "arranging your mind" to serve you. You no longer are a victim of any circumstance, but a Master of Creation on manifesting your heart's desire!

Believing you have a *Choice in everything* is one of the most important principles to hold. You could choose to feel hurt, betrayed, rejected, disrespected, abandoned, etc. Or you could choice to feel adored, honored, loved, appreciated, wanted and filled with JOY. The choice is *always* yours.

Everything that you need to be JOYful you have within you right now. *Stop* looking at the blocks... the reasons why not...the bad circumstances ...the person or people that are in your way. *Stop thinking, doing, saying or being anything that limits you...use your mind to surmount whatever is the matter.*

Expand your awareness to all the JOY in the world and the JOY-filled people living in it with you. Then use this conscious awareness to take responsibility for your personal choices and how all your experiences are there to ultimately serve your personal growth.

6. *Trust in your own personal power...*

When you believe and trust in the power of JOY and have the courage to follow your "North Star," it may look like a lot of forward and backward movements that is not getting you anywhere. But then one day, low and behold there you are~ smacked dab in the middle of your wildest dream~ and the only "real work" you did, was to Trust and Believe in yourself and the universe.

7.   *Live from Your Speak...*

When life challenges you and you forget "*Your Speak,*" (what is *your truth),* take a step back and examine all the emotions it brings up. If your thoughts are limiting you or making you feel fearful or scared, just stop what you are doing and begin to repeat, "*your empowering Speak*" until you get your Mojo back.

"My Speak" is... *Everything has a reason for being... Everything always works out in my favor... and I am blessed.* This absolutely believed truth always returns me to my center and a sense of peace. It brings me back to JOY. It reminds me that I am never doing anything alone. I've got a very powerful loving, protective, caring partner who never has and won't desert me now.

Recently I was asked "what's the difference between being filled with LOVE or JOY?" My answer was that even though you might have the intention of feeling pure *Love*, it still can cause pain for a multitude of reasons. But the emotion of *Joy* has no distractors. It's simply happiness and pleasure to the tenth degree.

When you filled with feelings of JOY, there is no room within your mind or body for upsets and pain. When you begin to get excited at the prospect of this new day as a fresh start to your life with magic and miracles yet to be discovered, everything changes in a flash!

Yes, it might be said that I am the eternal optimist, but I believe Johann Wolfgang von Goethe when he said, *"Whatever you do or dream you can do – begin it. Boldness has Genius and Power and MAGIC in it!"*

Once you seek out the Extraordinary in the ordinary, you will begin to create more JOY in your life than you've ever imagined. Anything ordinary will become Everything Extraordinary. Could you possibly ask for anything more? I don't think so!

En-JOY!

"Only by giving *are you able to receive* more *than you have."*

Jim Rohn

THE **JOY** of GIVING...

"One day a woman was walking along a stream and she found a precious stone glistening in the water. A little while later she met a traveler who said he was hungry, so the woman opened her bag to share her food.
The hungry traveler saw the precious stone and told the woman how much he would love to have it. She gave it to him without hesitation.

The traveler left with a full belly, rejoicing in his great fortune. He knew the stone was worth enough to give him security for a lifetime.

But a few days later he went in search of the woman to return the stone.

When he found her he said, "I've been thinking, I know how valuable the stone is you gave me and I think you have something even more valuable. I would like you to share with me what you have within that enabled you to so freely give me that stone. "

The woman smiled, "My pleasure, it's the Joy of Giving!"

   I am often asked, what makes you so JOYful? What is "it" that makes you so happy and smiling all the time? Well, I certainly could write a long list of "things" that most would agree are agreeable reasons for me to be so happy and filled with JOY. Many "things" people spend their lives working for or contriving to get so they can feel the way I feel. But, *my secret* for this non-stop bubbling stream of JOY that runs through my body, from my head to my toes, morning to night, doesn't come from "things," but *a way of being*. What I have is a deep true passion for the *JOY of Giving*.

I have learned that real JOY comes and never leaves, when you unselfishly give a piece of yourself. When you give to others from a genuine generosity, kindness, love caring, empathy, compassion and JOY, it opens up a channel for the kind of happiness that no one can ever take away from you. Permanent JOY and happiness results once you get past a silo mentality and expand yourself to feel the JOY in the difference only you can make in another person's life~ in all the big and little ways.

Giving to others always takes you out of yourself. You expand beyond your limitations. "It's impossible to create a better world without inner change that results from selfless service," said Deepak Chopra, "expansion of the self brings a direct experience of love, joy and all those other great emotions. Once you do, you'll get a glimpse of ecstasy, the state of standing outside yourself in the infinite field of Being that all the money in the world wouldn't buy a ticket back and you will want to be there forever. The mystery of giving is revealed only when you crave the ecstasy that has been glimpsed. Then a realization hits you with full force. I must give myself away. Without realizing it, you have been trying to do that all your life."

"Philanthropy: *The effort or inclination to increase the well-being of humankind,*" is a word that was coined over 2500 years ago in ancient Greece by the Aeschylus, as part of a myth woven around primitive creatures that were created to be human. The main character Prometheus received his "*philanthropos tropos*" or humanity-loving character by granting creatures two empowering life-changing gifts: First there was Fire, which symbolizing all knowledge, skills, technology, arts and science and then "Blind Hope" or Optimism. The two went together perfectly—with fire, humans could be optimistic; with optimism, they could use fire constructively to improve.

When I first read this my heart screamed out *YES, that's it!* I knew that my fire had been ignited with optimism long ago and that this Greek myth was actually based on truth. That each and every one of us has genetically inherited the same gifts Prometheus granted and has the power to use them. Whether we do or not, comes down to choice. So many people these day choose to live a *life less than* what they had hoped for, and the only thing that matters is how hard and long they can work, how much money and toys they can accumulate and if they are charitable, it's for the recognition. They believe that dreams are just dreams.

In one sense they are right; dreams are just dreams—guidebooks with roadmaps implanted in your being at birth, each leading you to your greatness. By following the signs of your calling, include difficult circumstances and rough terrains, dreams will soon become your life.

With all my heart I do believe that within each of us is the potential to live a beautiful life, beyond our wildest imagination. To experience a glimmer of greatness and to not only live out our dreams, but become even bigger and better within and because of them. Even though the words *powerful, great and big* mean different things to each of us...the comparison really doesn't matter. What does matter is that you decides what it means to you and then begins to live your life through those words and beliefs.

The common theme that runs through my life and all my work and certainly within these shared memoirs; to turn anything ordinary into everything Extraordinary is *always* Mind Over Matter. Because I am an ordinary woman who is living an Extraordinary life, without an endless supply of money or a full time staff taking care of my every whim and need, when I felt a great calling to stretch my philanthropic muscles so I could live an even more Extraordinary life, I sought out inspiration for designing a new paradigm that I found in my adored ninety-seven year old BFF, Betty Schoenbaum.

Betty is one of those blessed women who does have a fortune that she can and does give away with an open hand and heart to so many causes in the United States and Israel. But she taught me that even if she could only afford to give very little, the authentic caring and loving attention she gives to simply *everyone* she meets, is the greatest example of philanthropy as the actual word connotes: She is the perfect role-model for expressing the JOY of Giving and has made me a better person.

My dream was birthed from a moral hunger for *More*; more to be, more to do, more to give, more to loving and more to living a bigger fuller life. I believe that with the entrepreneurial energy that is emerging and being driven by new tools, pressures and a demand from "ordinary" people to do big things... even when money is scarce...the time has come when the average person like you and me has more power to make a difference than ever before. Being philanthropic is also about giving of your talents and time, not just money.

NOW, is the Time to Act. Today we must not think our way into a new way of acting; we must act our way into a new way of thinking ~ where giving with purpose can become the upside of the downside~ spreading joy, happiness and possibilities when and wherever we can. The time has come for all of us to redesign the business of benevolence where *The Joy of Giving*, of practicing being philanthropic to everyone with the same power I believe Prometheus intended, is the answer.

So if you are asking yourself, "How can I know *the Joy of Giving,* What can I do?" (I am so busy, have my own problems, no money, etc.)   I have a few suggestions.

1. Give of Yourself authentically and often.

As much as money is needed to fund research, etc., not a dime would be spent or make a bit of difference, if it were not sourced by open-hearted caring individuals. When you practice being authentically generous at all times in all sorts of circumstances, you will become part of the needed solution for improving our planet.

2. **Apply your talents to a social cause.**

Whatever you do for a living, whatever passions or hobbies you have perfected, there is a person or community organization that can use those talents to help make the world a better place. So many of you have many valuable skills that could be utilized for a good cause that would help to fill the gap that the loss of money has created. Even if you feel that you are already so busy, just a few hours a week can give you that sense of being philanthropic that is priceless. If you make or
do something that others can benefit from~ share your gifts. What will come back to you in the form of blessing, you can't even imagine!

3. **Become a Mentor.**

Offer your hard-earned wisdom to others in need of encouragement and guidance, anywhere from school kids, to graduates entering the workforce, to someone about to begin a new chapter in their life. Everyone has the qualifications to be a great mentor to someone, and the experience is just as rewarding for the mentor as the mentee. Structured or informally, sharing your wisdom and skills with one other person can eventually change the lives of thousands.

4. Become a Social Activist in your work.

Increasingly, more individuals and companies are concerned with practicing good citizenship. By thinking of ways you can start to help lead your fellow employees or associates, by being a more proactive citizen leader you can be the living example of Einstein's words; *"Power is the speed in which we convert possibilities into reality ~nothing can proceed until we move into the world of action."*

5. Become a Digital Citizen.

There are thousands of worthy organizations and charitable causes that use the Internet to engage support and mobilize resources and solicit ideas. You can support a charity you believe in or share information about a topic you are an expert on— all for the benefit of others and the Joy of Giving!

THE JOY OF GIVING in every form is the *"Secret Elixir"* for having a truly Extraordinary life! When you begin to live your life from service as opposed to self-serving, turning your everyday ordinary into everything extraordinary, will become as natural as the sun and the moon rising and setting each day.

Find your way to fill yourself up with JOY and then share that light and love with others. This is the fast track for living an Extraordinary life!

En-JOY!

LIFE ~ LUST ~ and **LOVE**...

HOW TO BE THE *SHERO*...
of Your Own Life Story!
My Gift Cheat Sheet

One of the things that I am doing on my "mission" to *JOYify* the world, is to lead workshops , retreats and large forums where groups of women and men can come together and work on the various issues in my books.

Below are the highlights of a workshop of *JOYification* that I create to further each woman's personal growth, a mini-refresher of the important points that I felt would help them become the real *Shero's* of their lives.

I guarantee you, that if you make a real commitment to applying these various concepts to anything ordinary, and truly believe in the depth of your heart that you can find your personal sweet spot of JOY, very soon, very very soon, they will become the foundation for your *Extraordinary Everything JOY-filled Life!*

En-*JOY!!*

LIFE ~ LUST ~ and **LOVE**...

First and Foremost...

THE FORMULA ~ The Art of Living Well!

- *By the Thoughts That You Focus on...*
- *By the Words That You Speak...*
- *By Your Actions and Reactions...*
- *And Whether or Not You Believe...*
  You Deserve To Have What You Really Want...
  Is How You Create The Experience and the Quality
  of Your Life.

Once you begin to take responsibility for using each
piece of The Formula positively focused~ that every
single man and women in the world uses every single
moment of their day to create their lives~ and it will
become impossible for you *not* to have a JOY filled
Extraordinary life!

Reframe Thoughts that don't serve you!

Reframing, takes a thought~ in the context of an
opinion, judgment or belief that brings you any form
of discomfort or dissatisfaction~ and turns it around so
that "the positive reflective side" now faces the situation
and every sense that is being activated by the negative
thought can now be *En-lightened* to serve your higher
self!

Become a Master of Creation!

A Master of Creation recognizes that *The Formula* is how you create the quality of Your Life. Once you become consciously aware of how you are using the steps~ positively or negatively~ take responsibility for whether they are serving you or not, and if not, mentally return to all of your peak experiences to empower you in your next moment of choices~ A Master of Creating an Extraordinary Joy-filled life will become your everyday "ordinary" life!

My Three Fav's...
for staying centered and get back on course.

1. *You are either In or You are Out*." What do you believe...What is Your "Speak" about The Source and who you are? Think about that a moment before you answer honestly. Because, either you believe what you say and live from that belief, or you don't, which would makes you a major BS'er! My "Speak/ Truth" is that *Everything has a reason for being... Everything always works out in my favor... and... I am blessed."* When I am feeling fearful or tenuous about anything, I stop and ask myself, *"are you in or are you out?"* The truth will set you free.

2. *Create Affirming Rituals*. When you take right actions in the direction of your intentions, in the form of repeating an action that reaffirms your intentions to see you/your life a certain way, these affirming rituals will be reaffirming with yourself and The Universe...*this is the only way I intend to live my life!* Whether it is a

morning beach walk or a hour at the gym, listening to a CD or reading the bible, eating particular foods, etc., anything you see as affirming your intentions works!

3. *Listen to Your Body~ Answer the Call~*
It has been scientifically proven that dis-ease is caused by all the toxins continuously put into our bodies, Mentally and Physically. You may be unconscious to what you are doing...but your body isn't. So listen carefully when it tells you something is wrong ... Answer the call with right thoughtful actions. Soon whispers of perfect health will be the new message.

Find Your Life Purpose...

We all have a special calling that is nestled within our hearts and it reveals itself through the things that bring us the greatest joy and ignite our passion. Work is no longer work and the course of action to realize your dreams becomes an exciting adventure.

The same message is true for creating a sexy booty! You do what you need to do to get the results you want from the joy and passion for seeing and having the positive end-result. As for *Your Life Purpose*, all that The Source of it all requires of you is 4 things:

1. Be Happy~ Know true JOY~ Love Enough... *Ask yourself, am I having fun yet?*

2. Discover what just *YOU* were created to do... *Stop... Look... Listen.*

3. Dare to Dream... *Fearlessly Reach for Your Heart-Held Dream.*

4. Become your version of someone you admire the most~ *Emulate Role-Models and Mentors*

How to Avoid & Eliminate Toxic Relationships

Unfortunately there are lots of damage human beings running around these days and even more unfortunate is they seem to need to regurgitate their pain on others in a myriad of ways. Once you are able to spot the signs of these narcissist master manipulators early on, even if you slip and enter into their silken web, you will be able to slip out much sooner with just the slightest damage.

Abusers practice Gas-Lighting. Making you feel as if you are crazy when they accuse you of doing just the opposite of what you did or who they said they were.

Abusers tend to blame others for their short-comings. As if what they did is all Your Fault, then they say or do something hurtful or abusive.

Abusers instill fear and defensiveness in you by attempting to try to intimidate you with violent behavior, dominance or power tactics to control.

Abusers tend to abuse substances and then lie about using them. This can often be hidden so you have no idea, but somewhere in their actions will be a sign.

Abusers often use gifts, goodies and heartfelt apologizes to smooth over past actions and to lower your resistance to being abused again.

Abusers are very controlling and often get physical after verbally or emotionally abusing.

Abusers often only want you for themselves and demand all your attention as much in a day or week as is possible, and then get angry "because it's not enough."

Abusers will punish you for the time away or given to someone else. There is no way to ever give enough, so little or big punishments come often.

Individuals that are "inflicted" with narcissism are master manipulators and tend to abuse the people in their lives in one way another. But now you know what to look for before you become another "victim of circumstances" of a toxic abusive situation. Always remember, no matter how nice the package looks, if something *feels* wrong, walk away.

How to Play The Player...and Win!

Playing the Player means that if a man comes into your life and offers you all forms of delight, but clearly is not marriage or long-term relationship material~ Be smart, have fun and enjoy all the gifts (someone is going to, why not you?)...Just Don't Give Him Your Heart! He's not necessarily a bad guy he is just a player (so play). He is not a keeper. Remember, only keepers get to have your heart!

How to Fall Madly in Love with Yourself...
Attract true love!

One thing I know for sure is that once you truly can love yourself completely, you send out a light that attracts back to you friends and lovers who are capable of loving you the way you deserve to be loved. *But if you don't love all your nooks and crannies, why would anyone else?* You want to choose who is in your life, not accept whomever is there as a default option.

How do you do that? Take all those feeling of Love and acceptance that you have so lovingly given to others, and give it fully and honestly to yourself. Treat yourself like the most important person in the world by giving yourself all the good things you are looking to come from someone else~ compliments, flowers and gifts, acknowledgment, acceptance, kindness, approval, and mostly, unconditional love.

Go to your memory bank and conjure up your best and most pride-worthy self, because that's still who you are today...no matter what "your reality" looks like. Then ask *the You* of twenty=five years ago what kind of person you had hoped you would be twenty-five years later-today. I bet you will be surprised at how much you are like that wishful image, maybe even better, now LOVE the YOU, you've discovered!

How to be an Ageless beauty for decades!

Here are my absolute best tips, garnered from some truly amazing ageless beauties. Each one is intended to "lift and pump up everything" to give you a sense of confidence in all of you.

1. Consider yourself an Ageless Beauty today and truly believe that you can be an object of love and desire throughout your entire life! How you act and think about yourself will be reflected back by how others see and treat you. Always be self-confident. Just don't make the mistake of pretending you are forever twenty-five!

2. Exhibit Self-reliance. It's very appealing when others sense that your choices in all situations come from trusting that you can handle whatever.

3. Inhabit your body completely. Every shape has its own unique curves and delights, create your own signature way of moving with confidence.

4. Use your refined mind to become an interesting and interested woman~ A great conversationalist is very attractive to all species.

5. Create Your Own Unique Style...beyond trends or someone else's opinion. Be your own work of art!

6. Be Adventurous...and fully embrace each moment of the day. Fill yourself up with all things that bring you JOY and share your happiness. You will become like honey to the bees...and flowers to the butterflies!

7. Own Your Magnificence... and *Light Up Every Room!!* If you want to be the kind of rare jewel worthy of love, adoration and well taken special care of, you must develop a powerful belief and ownership of *Your Own Magnificence*... which can only be generated from the inside out.

See yourself as such a rare gem,.. a one of a kind...truly priceless if put up for auction... there is No One Else in The Entire World like you! How valuable is that? Yep... Priceless!

   Treat yourself as if you are Priceless Valuable and Unique...and so will the rest of the world! With a light that shines so bright on every single part of you leave no doubt as to your own self-worth, self-esteem or self-respect.

Owning Your Magnificence without any false pride or arrogance is simply acknowledging how special you are and the realization that anyone who has you in their life is darn lucky!

   Above and beyond all the messages I want you receive from all my work is this...

   This is Your Life, Your Own Production, Your Novella, and you are meant to be The SHERO of your Own Life Story. You are a Master of your Creation and no one else has any rights or should have any say in what you chose to do or not do, be or not be, whether to feel good or bad, right or wrong. The decisions and the responsibility for your choices are all yours.

Last but as you all know... not least...

JOY ~ JOY ~ JOY

Everything I do... my life and philanthropy work, my moment to moment interactions and thoughts ...my reason for being... are all because I really truly believe that my "job" is to be *The Source of Life showing up as JOY.* It is my highest commitment and what I base all my thinking, choices and decisions upon.

Not because of some wonderful altruistic reason they make movies about, but between you and me (our little secret, ok?) quite selfish reasons: It just feels so darn good to have the amazing energy of JOY flowing throughout my body 24/7!

Yes, of course I am human and fearful thoughts and crappy feelings do sneak in sometimes. Just like everyone else, I do feel pain, disappointment, frustrations, upsets, and sadness and have been known to wallow in my misery for a certain amount of time. But these emotions are only permitted to invade my sacred space for just so long and then I do whatever I can to flush them out as quickly as possible.

Because JOY is my highest commitment, I go in search as soon as humanly possible for the beautiful rainbow in the clouds. Once I find it, I practice reframing my ideas and thoughts till they serve me. Then I go merrily on my way!

Sometimes that's hard to do and happens later than sooner... instead of the other way around. But since I am firmly rooted in my commitment to being and having a JOY-filled life, I now can relax and trust in the process, knowing, that I will be just fine again and JOY will be my reality once more.

Besides the fact that it feels so good to be filled with JOY and love instead of fear and doubts, it's really the best skin care treatment available for glowing wrinkle blurring results! It's also a world class fighter against dis-eases like stress and anxiety...which are the major killers to good health and feeling ageless.

Making JOY your highest commitment can serve you as well as it has served me. It simply is saying that no matter what life throws at you, you are committed to getting back to a peaceful, centered, more JOYful place, sooner than later. You know you have control over your thoughts and feelings and can begin whenever you want to start to see your life through a clearer different lens.

I could go on for hours on this one... but you can read more about it in any and all my books. All I want to say for now, is now that you know how it works you can no longer pretend (in any area of your life) that you are a "victim of circumstances" for having a JOY-filled life!

If making a difference in the world matters to you, then you need to admit that the only way you will really make a difference in this toxic world is to consistently be a piece of the light reflecting all the darkness. When you send love where there is hate and prejudice, compassion and empathy for others that may have hurt you or don't know any better, when you can forgive yourselves for "Staying too long or making uneducated choices from need instead of want," you will truly be *owning your magnificence,* and your *Shero* life story will be your prize possession.

YOU and Me~ Him and Her... we all are doing the best we can with what we know and have at this very moment in time. That doesn't mean you have to accept anything or be with anyone that doesn't serve you or your highest good... or bring you JOY. But now that you know how it works, you can no longer take any of it personally or let it hurt you anymore.

Other people's actions are *never* about you...they are *always* about them. Once you truly get that, in this bright new shiny moment you can and will do better, feel better, act better, choose better and use this new knowledge to create a bigger better life. You can now use your newly gained powers to walk away and reframe what no longer serves you~ including your negative beliefs and thoughts~ and positively use The Formula to set you straight in the direction of your best life yet!

En-JOY!

"If one advances confidently in the direction of his dreams, and endeavors to live the life which he has imagined, he will meet with a success unexpected in common hours."

Henry David Thoreau

CLOSING THOUGHTS

Opening up my private journal and sharing my secret memoirs with "strangers" was something I certainly never intended to do. These entries were made only to be used for my personal growth, to help keep me on course when my limiting humanness would sneak in and overtake my "wise inner knowing" self. It's always been my private "go to" refresher course when life's "challenges and opportunities for growth" come calling.

But, as my audience continued to grow and I saw that the core message behind my work was resonating with so many women and men, I felt compelled to give even more. The timing felt right for me to finally open up my own personal tool kit for "turning *anything ordinary into Everything Extraordinary,*" which is exactly how I approach things. To realize my intention to help transform the toxic energy in the world into a global energy of compassion kindness, love and JOY, sharing the wisdom of my "mentors" was an important step.

From my first words to these very last few, my heart message is the same: Each and every one of you has the power within to create a JOY-filled Extraordinary Life. I know first-hand, that no matter what the challenges, circumstances or personal trials and tribulations that may test your fortitude or perseverance, if you believe in yourself, anything is possible.

Maybe not in this moment, or even for a lot more moments, but once you are willing to take responsibility for your thoughts, words, actions and reactions, and whether or not you believe you deserve to have the quality of life you want and deserve (positively abiding by The Formula), a JOY filled Extraordinary Life will absolutely be your reality. As with gratitude, it's a practice. But as we all know, practice makes perfect!

Arianna Huffington, Oprah Winfrey and Wayne Dyer, to name a few more of my mentors and role models I so respect and admire, also see the process of accessing the power of your thoughts through *observation, contemplation and then choice.*

To first *observe* your thoughts to see and feel if they are expanding or limiting you, then to *contemplate* the negative and the positive results that come from those thoughts and to finally make a *choice* which to follow and which version of those thoughts best serve you, is the way to a JOY-filled healthy abundant life.

I truly hope that the vignettes and stories you've read in my "secret memoirs" have stimulated the process of observing the thoughts that are directing your life, and in turn have encouraged you to slow down to take the time to contemplate and choose rightly to follow the ones that serve you in having a healthy JOY-filled Extraordinary life. "I wondered why someone didn't do something~ then I realized, I am someone."

Joy

All ABOUT JOY...

 Like so many others, I began my illustrious career by simply falling into it. When I was just a sweet young thing my adored father, an extremely talented and highly touted photographer, passed away, leaving a studio and a challenge.

As a single mom and former model driven to stretch my creative genes, I took up the study of photography and reopened the studio. I slowly began to create my own signature "moody black and white portraits that masterfully capture a person's essence" and was soon discovered by the senior editor of *The Philadelphia Magazine,* who chose to do a four page expo on my photographs in their yearly "Keeper Issue." This fortuitous meeting jump-started a very exciting nationally acclaimed career with a celebrity clientele that lasted for years.

In retrospect, all of my creative career choices have been fueled by the desire to awaken others to their outer and inner beauty and to understand and utilize the life-changing emotion of JOY. So the most natural segue was into television, where I went on to create and host a cable television show called *Catch The JOY* that was based on finding positive solutions to potentially negative everyday problems.

Encouraged by so many positive experiences and a natural restlessness, I expanded my creative talents into the written word that fortunately was embraced whole-heartedly. My first book, *How an Ordinary Woman Can Have an Extraordinary Life: The Formula for The Art of Living Well* turned out to be an international Best Seller, produced in 14 languages in 22 countries!

This was followed by *How an Ordinary Guy can Become an Extraordinary Man,* and a bit later by *It's Just a Game~ It's all in how you play it: A Travelholics Search for Life's Simple Secrets and the Dessert du Jour;* A delicious book on the joy of Five Star Travel. Now with *LIFE~LUST and LOVE,* an exciting new chapter has begun.

As a Motivational Speaker and Workshop Leader, with my work available in E-book's and virtual video and audio series, I've been able to share my work in various places around the world. As a Communications and marketing consultant to businesses, organizations and medical offices, as well as a coach and mentor, I am living my dream of inspiring others to live the life they desire and were meant to live.

Yet with all my varied accomplishments, I will always feel as if my greatest achievements have been in all the loving and caring relationships I have developed with my family, friends and diverse communities.

Through my private foundation, *Pay It Forward Angels Network,* I am able to give my inspirational

books for free to women in need and now as the
champion *The Circle of Community Partnership.org*,
I am helping to spread more awareness to the joy of
giving throughout the community. Through it all, my
intention is to help others find their voice, their power
and that sweet peaceful spot within themselves.

As a passionate explorer, I now split my time between
Florida, and depending on my mood or the weather,
wherever the next adventure takes me. But since life
is The Adventure, my willingness and passport are
always ready for whatever the universe grand plan.
Hopefully, I will get a chance to meet you, my beloved
readers, along the way and give you a hug. Until then...

En-JOY!

If you are looking to get more JOY in your life or the life of your business, etc., you certainly came to the right place! Below are the various communication services that I provide for varied businesses, medical groups, corporations, organizations and individuals.

For more detailed information please visit my web site or call me directly to schedule a time for us to meet and discuss your particular needs. Either way, I will definitely look forward to hearing from you.

www.JoyWeston.com

Joy@JoyWeston.com

1-941-227-5336

- Communications Consultant
- Attraction Marketer for your target audience
- "Compliments of"...Customized Gift Books
- Relationship and Personal Coach/ Mentor
- International Best Selling Author
- Motivational Speaker * Workshop Presenter
- Internal Communications ~ Team Trainer